WORLD HISTORY

Auschwitz

David Robson

LUCENT BOOKS

A part of Gale, Cengage Learning

GALE
CENGAGE Learning

Detroit • New York • San Francisco • New Haven, Conn • Waterville, Maine • London

GALE
CENGAGE Learning™

LIBRARY OF CONGRESS CATALOGING-IN-PUBLICATION DATA

Robson, David.
   Auschwitz / by David Robson.
      p. cm. -- (World history)
   Includes bibliographical references and index.
   ISBN 978-1-4205-0131-5 (hardcover)
   1. Auschwitz (Concentration camp)--Juvenile literature. 2. Birkenau (Concentration camp)--Juvenile literature. 3. Jews--Persecutions--Europe--Juvenile literature. 4. Holocaust, Jewish (1939–1945)--Juvenile literature. I. Title.
   D805.5.A96R63 2009
   940.53'1853858--dc22
                                                    2008052817

Lucent Books
27500 Drake Rd.
Farmington Hills, MI 48331

ISBN-13: 978-1-4205-0131-5
ISBN-10: 1-4205-0131-3

Printed in the United States of America
2 3 4 5 6 7 13 12 11 10 09

Contents

Foreword

Each year, on the first day of school, nearly every history teacher faces the task of explaining why his or her students should study history. Many reasons have been given. One is that lessons exist in the past from which contemporary society can benefit and learn. Another is that exploration of the past allows us to see the origins of our customs, ideas, and institutions. Concepts such as democracy, ethnic conflict, or even things as trivial as fashion or mores, have historical roots.

Reasons such as these impress few students, however. If anything, these explanations seem remote and dull to young minds. Yet history is anything but dull. And therein lies what is perhaps the most compelling reason for studying history: History is filled with great stories. The classic themes of literature and drama—love and sacrifice, hatred and revenge, injustice and betrayal, adversity and overcoming adversity—fill the pages of history books, feeding the imagination as well as any of the great works of fiction do.

The story of the Children's Crusade, for example, is one of the most tragic in history. In 1212 Crusader fever hit Europe. A call went out from the pope that all good Christians should journey to Jerusalem to drive out the hated Muslims and return the city to Christian control. Heeding the call, thousands of children made the journey. Parents bravely allowed many children to go, and entire communities were inspired by the faith of these small Crusaders. Unfortunately, many boarded ships captained by slave traders, who enthusiastically sold the children into slavery as soon as they arrived at their destination. Thousands died from disease, exposure, and starvation on the long march across Europe to the Mediterranean Sea. Others perished at sea.

Another story, from a modern and more familiar place, offers a soul-wrenching view of personal humiliation but also the ability to rise above it. Hatsuye Egami was one of 110,000 Japanese Americans sent to internment camps during World War II. "Since yesterday we Japanese have ceased to be human beings," he wrote in his diary. "We are numbers. We are no longer Egamis, but the number 23324. A tag with that number is on every trunk, suitcase and bag. Tags, also, on our breasts." Despite such dehumanizing treatment, most internees worked hard to control their bitterness. They created workable communities inside the camps and demonstrated again and again their loyalty as Americans.

These are but two of the many stories from history that can be found in the pages of the Lucent Books World History series. All World History titles rely on sound research and verifiable evidence, and all give students a clear sense of time, place, and chronology through maps and timelines as well as text.

All titles include a wide range of authoritative perspectives that demonstrate the complexity of historical interpretation and sharpen the reader's critical thinking skills. Formally documented quotations and annotated bibliographies enable students to locate and evaluate sources, often instantaneously via the Internet, and serve as valuable tools for further research and debate.

Finally, Lucent's World History titles present rousing good stories, featuring vivid primary source quotations drawn from unique, sometimes obscure sources such as diaries, public records, and contemporary chronicles. In this way, the voices of participants and witnesses as well as important biographers and historians bring the study of history to life. As we are caught up in the lives of others, we are reminded that we too are characters in the ongoing human saga, and we are better prepared for our own roles.

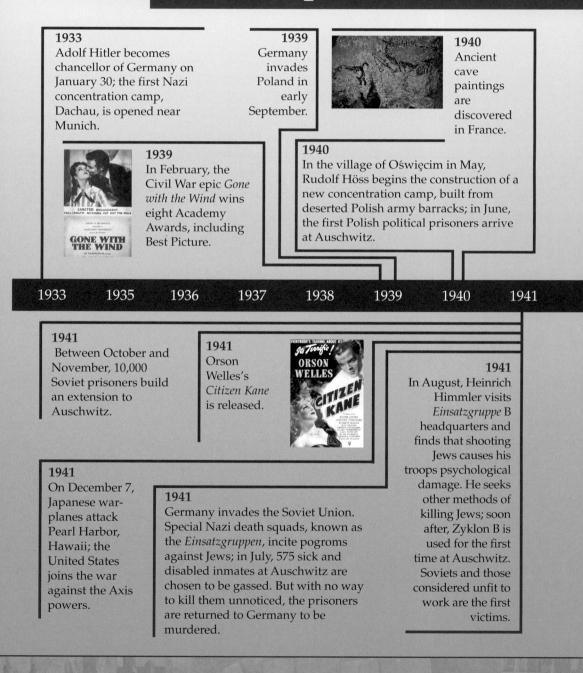

1933
Adolf Hitler becomes chancellor of Germany on January 30; the first Nazi concentration camp, Dachau, is opened near Munich.

1939
Germany invades Poland in early September.

1940
Ancient cave paintings are discovered in France.

1939
In February, the Civil War epic *Gone with the Wind* wins eight Academy Awards, including Best Picture.

1940
In the village of Oświęcim in May, Rudolf Höss begins the construction of a new concentration camp, built from deserted Polish army barracks; in June, the first Polish political prisoners arrive at Auschwitz.

| 1933 | 1935 | 1936 | 1937 | 1938 | 1939 | 1940 | 1941 |

1941
Between October and November, 10,000 Soviet prisoners build an extension to Auschwitz.

1941
Orson Welles's *Citizen Kane* is released.

1941
In August, Heinrich Himmler visits *Einsatzgruppe* B headquarters and finds that shooting Jews causes his troops psychological damage. He seeks other methods of killing Jews; soon after, Zyklon B is used for the first time at Auschwitz. Soviets and those considered unfit to work are the first victims.

1941
On December 7, Japanese war-planes attack Pearl Harbor, Hawaii; the United States joins the war against the Axis powers.

1941
Germany invades the Soviet Union. Special Nazi death squads, known as the *Einsatzgruppen*, incite pogroms against Jews; in July, 575 sick and disabled inmates at Auschwitz are chosen to be gassed. But with no way to kill them unnoticed, the prisoners are returned to Germany to be murdered.

Time of Auschwitz

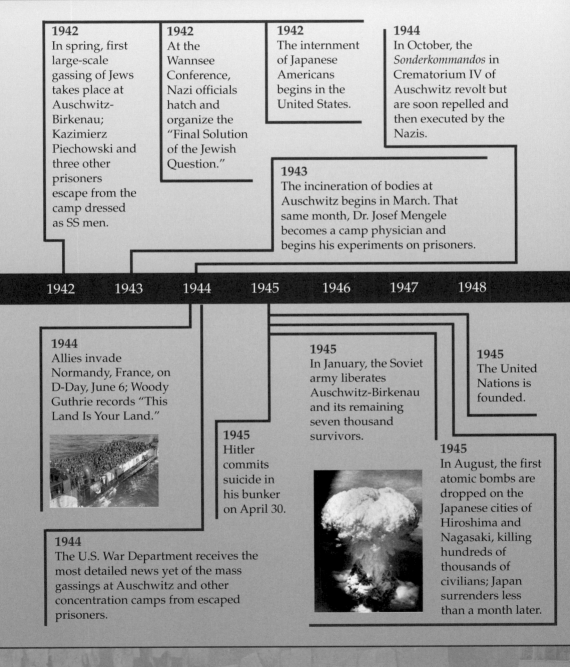

1942
In spring, first large-scale gassing of Jews takes place at Auschwitz-Birkenau; Kazimierz Piechowski and three other prisoners escape from the camp dressed as SS men.

1942
At the Wannsee Conference, Nazi officials hatch and organize the "Final Solution of the Jewish Question."

1942
The internment of Japanese Americans begins in the United States.

1944
In October, the *Sonderkommandos* in Crematorium IV of Auschwitz revolt but are soon repelled and then executed by the Nazis.

1943
The incineration of bodies at Auschwitz begins in March. That same month, Dr. Josef Mengele becomes a camp physician and begins his experiments on prisoners.

| 1942 | 1943 | 1944 | 1945 | 1946 | 1947 | 1948 |

1944
Allies invade Normandy, France, on D-Day, June 6; Woody Guthrie records "This Land Is Your Land."

1945
In January, the Soviet army liberates Auschwitz-Birkenau and its remaining seven thousand survivors.

1945
The United Nations is founded.

1945
Hitler commits suicide in his bunker on April 30.

1945
In August, the first atomic bombs are dropped on the Japanese cities of Hiroshima and Nagasaki, killing hundreds of thousands of civilians; Japan surrenders less than a month later.

1944
The U.S. War Department receives the most detailed news yet of the mass gassings at Auschwitz and other concentration camps from escaped prisoners.

"Reckoning"

In January 1959 German attorney general Fritz Bauer received a surprising letter. The contents spoke of records from Auschwitz, a known Nazi concentration camp during World War II. The records, only recently discovered, included the names of thousands of people executed at the camp and their murderers. Signed by the camp commander, the lists provided detailed proof of the many atrocities committed at Auschwitz between 1940 and 1945.

The world had already witnessed the trial and execution of defeated Nazi political and military leaders who were tried as war criminals in Nuremberg in 1945 or in Kraków in 1947 in what was known in Poland as the Auschwitz trial. But Bauer pursued the new information; for the next four years he built cases against twenty-two additional defendants, and five days before Christmas 1963, the Frankfurt Auschwitz Trial, also called "the second Auschwitz trial," began.

Before the start of the trial, Bauer spoke to reporters: "If our Auschwitz trial is to make sense . . . then it should be as a warning and a lesson for us. The trial must demonstrate to the world that our new German Republic is a democracy which is determined to preserve the dignity of every individual."[1]

The preservation of dignity for many citizens was not a given in the German Republic in the era of the Third Reich, a period of only twelve years, from 1933 to 1945. During this period German dictator Adolf Hitler and his Nazi Party attempted to exterminate the Jews of Europe through systematic, state-sponsored mass murder. The Third Reich was a totalitarian regime—asserting total control over all aspects of society—that targeted many other so-called enemies of the Reich for persecution or extermination, including Gypsies, homosexuals, the mentally and physically disabled, Communists, and political critics. The most notorious symbol of Nazi brutality was its network of concentration camps within Germany, such as Dachau and Buchenwald, and the six extermination camps in occupied Poland—Belzec, Chelmno, Majdanek, Sobibor, Treblinka, and the the largest of all, Auschwitz— where prisoners and slave laborers were forced to live and work in subhuman conditions or, more often, were simply transported to be killed.

As a former concentration camp prisoner who escaped to Denmark, Fritz Bauer knew firsthand the brutality of the Nazis and their single-minded goal of extermination. When he returned to Germany in 1945, he spent almost two decades seeking out war criminals. With his black-rimmed glasses and ever-present cigarette, Bauer was intent on justice.

As the trial date approached in the winter of 1963, 210 former Auschwitz prisoners flew to Frankfurt to confront their past. Eighteen years after the end of World War II, many were still feeling the deepest scars of the conflict. And now they were about to face the Auschwitz officers and guards responsible for their captivity and torture.

The Frankfurt Trial lasted for nearly two years and became the most significant trial in German history. In all, 430 hours of testimony were recorded, 319 witnesses were called, and each day brought the latest trial headlines to the rest of the world. It appeared a reckoning was at hand.

What Was Auschwitz?

Auschwitz was located 31 miles (50km) west of Kraków, in occupied Poland. Formerly an army barracks site, the camp was opened in 1940 as a prison for Polish criminals and prisoners of war. By

This is one of many gas chambers used throughout Poland during the Holocaust.

the time Allied forces liberated it in 1945 it had become a sprawling complex of some forty sub-camps, infamous as a death camp. During his testimony at the Nuremberg Trials, Auschwitz commandant Rudolf Höss estimated that almost 3 million people died there.

Historians have since adjusted that number to between 1.1 and 1.6 million deaths. Of these victims, 960,000, or 90 percent, were Jewish. Others murdered include 74,000 non-Jewish Poles; 21,000 Gypsies; 15,000 Soviets; and 10,000 to 15,000 Czechs, French, Germans, Austrians, and Yugoslavs. Over 200,000 of those who perished were children.

While hundreds of thousands of people died from starvation, disease, and individual violence, most perished in Nazi execution chambers designed specifically for mass murder.

To carry out their extermination plan, the Nazis deported their victims to concentration or death camps, herded most of them into makeshift shower rooms, sealed the windows and doors, and pumped Zyklon B, a deadly gas, into the chamber, killing those inside in a matter of minutes. This assembly line of death continued as bodies were moved into crematoria, where large ovens turned the still warm corpses into ash.

Although Auschwitz was only one of dozens of concentration and death camps spread throughout Poland, Germany, and other European countries, it became the most notorious. The Holocaust—the state-sponsored slaughter of over 6 million Jews and 6 to 8 million Russians, Gypsies, and other Europeans under Hitler—is widely considered the twentieth century's most horrendous, and in its scope, most incomprehensible, crime against humanity.

Why Was It Important?

Auschwitz was an essential part of the Nazis' "Final Solution," a secret plan that called for the total extermination of Jews from Europe. The ideas that led to the "Final Solution" and camps such as Auschwitz had deep roots in European history but were developed by Hitler and his National Socialist German Workers' Party. Hitler cultivated German anti-Semitism and encouraged mass hysteria about the dangers presented by people of Jewish heritage. To the extent that he succeeded in implementing his plan, Auschwitz stands as a reminder of the dangers of totalitarianism and the power of propaganda, and represents perhaps the greatest atrocity in recorded history.

For survivors and their families, Auschwitz stands as testimony to their suffering but also to their will to live, their adaptability in the face of destruction, and their sense of responsibility to make sure the tragedy is neither forgotten nor repeated.

What Can It Teach Us Today?

Auschwitz remains the site of the largest mass murder in recorded history. But despite the near universal outrage at the genocide committed there and at other death camps, and despite the thousands

Although the global community was outraged by what took place at Auschwitz, genocide has continued. Tutsi tribe members killed by Hutus in Africa is a recent example.

of memorials built to commemorate the murder of so many people, genocide has recurred in the world. In 1994, for example, eight hundred thousand members of the Tutsi tribe in the African nation of Rwanda were systematically slaughtered by their Hutu countrymen. And beginning in 2003 Janjaweed militias began killing and raping Sudanese citizens in the Darfur region of their country. The forces that produced the Holocaust—prejudice, hatred, greed, abuse of power—are still at work. A study of Auschwitz is a reminder that the threat of genocide remains a serious danger now and in the future.

Chapter One

Ashes to Ashes: The Origins of the "Final Solution"

Historians agree that it is virtually impossible to pinpoint the exact moment when high-ranking officials of the Nazi (National Socialist German Workers') Party decided to murder the Jews of Europe in a plan they called the "Final Solution." What is beyond dispute is how successful they were in achieving this insidious goal and how unrepentant many of them were about it. According to historian Laurence Rees, Adolf Eichmann, one of the Holocaust's architects, said that "the knowledge of having participated in the murder of millions of Jews gave him such satisfaction that he would 'jump laughingly into his grave.'"[2]

Both the design and implementation of the Holocaust, also known by the Hebrew word "Shoah," evolved over a number of years and hinged on thousands of decisions—large and small—made by scores of people. Rees writes that these individuals, from Nazi commanders to low-level infantrymen to ordinary German citizens, "each made the decision not just to take part but to contribute initiatives in order to solve the problem of how to kill human beings and dispose of their bodies on a scale never attempted before."[3]

What linked these groups was belief in the cause of German nationalism and deep-seated hatred of the Jewish people. Both factors had been a destructive force in European history for centuries before the Holocaust.

Jewish Persecution in Europe

The persecution of Jews corresponds with the rise of Christianity in the Roman Empire, associated with Christian portrayals of Jews as the murderers of Jesus of Nazareth. Although the Old Testament claims the Jews as God's chosen people, Jewish European history has been marked by eras of violent persecution and exile ever since. As the Christian Church established itself as the most powerful institution in Europe, Jews and other minority groups were targeted as the enemies of Christianity. In the seventh century Jews were driven from Spain. During the Crusades, which extended through the eleventh, twelfth, and thirteenth centuries, they were killed by the thousands in Germany. A century later Jews were blamed for the plague outbreaks that devastated Europe and were consequently banished from many communities. By the 1400s persecution by the Inquisition of the Church left Jews impoverished and vulnerable to violent purges, or pogroms. Such treatment continued in Russia in the 1800s and early 1900s.

Despite this castigation and their limited opportunities, Jews remained vital to European communities as laborers, politicians, businesspeople, and taxpayers. And by the mid-nineteenth century their numbers were growing again, especially in Europe. In Austria alone, between 1850 and 1910 the Jewish population of Vienna grew from 6,000 to 175,000. Germany's fortunes were rising, too. In 1871, through

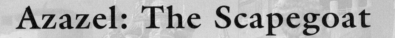

Azazel: The Scapegoat

According to the Old Testament, ancient Hebrews observed Yom Kippur—the Day of Atonement—by driving a goat, or "azazel," into the wilderness: "And the Goat shall bear upon him all their iniquities unto a Land not inhabited." This symbolic ritual, the Jews believed, cleansed the community and allowed them to prosper. But over the millennia, the scapegoat came to be seen as a person who is blamed for the sins of others. During the rise of the Third Reich, Jews were often blamed for Germany's economic and social problems. Art, music, and books were filled with anti-Semitic propaganda, and lurid publications such as the magazine *Der Stürmer* portrayed Jews as subhuman and murderous. The day after the brutal violence of Kristallnacht, the magazine's publisher, Julius Streicher, spoke before a crowd of one hundred thousand people. In his speech, Streicher heaped the evils of history onto the shoulders of Jews everywhere: "Our hope," he said, "is that the Jewish people will one day receive the penalty they deserve for all the sorrow, misery, and trouble they have brought the peoples. Then the world will breathe more easily, and there will be peace." Under the oppressive Nazi regime, the biblical scapegoaters became the scapegoats themselves.

Lev. 16:22 (King James Version).
Quoted in Randall L. Bytwerk, *Landmark Speeches of National Socialism.* College Station: Texas A&M University Press, 2008, p. 92.

a combination of diplomacy and warfare, chief minister Otto von Bismarck unified the thirty-nine separate states within German territory into one. For almost fifty years, the German empire's laws, politics, and economics were linked. The nation led the world as an industrial power, its strength virtually unrivaled in Europe.

But soon, powerful political rivalries would plunge all of Europe into war and European Jews would be on the defensive once again.

"Racially Inferior"

World War I, a global conflict pitting the Central Powers (led by Germany, Austria-Hungary, and the Ottoman Empire of the Turks) against the Allies (led by the British Empire, Russia, France, Italy, and the United States), devastated the continent for four years, beginning in 1914. The conflict killed over 20 million soldiers and civilians, injured 20 million more, and tore apart an entire generation. Although anti-Semitism—the hatred of Jewish people—and prejudice began generations before, World War I brought discrimination and the casting of blame into sharper focus.

Jews in Austria and Germany had initially been caught up in the war effort as proud citizens of the Rhineland. Thousands volunteered and fought in World War I, and approximately twelve thousand of them died in the service of their country. But as Germany began losing the war, Jews were accused of undermining the country. According to writer Ian Kershaw, "Jews were now at-

tacked as racially inferior . . . and as shirkers avoiding service at the front."[4] As the nearly defeated nation looked for scapegoats to blame for their humiliating loss, Jews, despite their proven patriotism, became an easy target. So, too, did the civilian leaders and Marxist politicians responsible for the terms of the treaty ending the war, which imposed harsh conditions on the defeated nations, especially Germany.

The Treaty of Versailles, signed on June 28, 1919, officially ended World War I. Its key clauses placed the entire blame for the war on Germany, ordered the dismantling of Germany's armed forces and the ceding of territory to Russia and France, and required Germany to pay billions of dollars in war reparations to the victorious Allies. The Weimar (German) politicians who accepted these terms by signing the treaty—labeled "November Criminals" in the German press—were, like the Jews, considered traitors to their nation.

The Rebirth of German Nationalism

Postwar Germany was a nation in ruins. The new, postwar government, led by the German Social Democrats, remained mostly ineffective between 1919 and 1932. Jobs were few, poverty rose, and a national feeling of despair and humiliation descended on the once proud country. Germany, says biographer Ian Kershaw, "was an empire wracked by modern nationalist and ethnic conflict, ill at ease with itself, struggling to cope with new social and political forces pulling it apart, decaying. . . . Germans felt their culture, way of life, living standards, and status under threat."[5]

The stage was set for the rise of an ideology, and a leader, that promised to restore Germany's wealth and greatness. The leader was Austrian-born Adolf Hitler, a failed art student, anti-Semite, and decorated Bavarian corporal during World War I. Historian Robert Wohl says that Hitler's time in the army was "the happiest period of his life because he had finally found a group to which he belonged . . . a group that he admired."[6] After the war, Hitler found his political voice among a group of disaffected rabble-rousers in Munich

Adolf Hitler, top row, far right, is shown with his Linz, Austria, high school class around 1904.

who called themselves the National Socialist Workers' Party, or Nazi Party.

In 1920 Hitler and his closest aides developed a twenty-five-point program by which the Nazi Party would operate, including the promotion of religious freedom, the right to self-determination, and the forging of a party that confronted the perceived Jewish menace head-on. Hitler envisioned not simply a form of government but an empire that would live for a thousand years.

Hitler coined the term Third Reich as a way of connecting Germany's past to the present. The First Reich, also known as the Holy Roman Empire of the German Nation, began in 800 with the crowning of Charlemagne and ended with the abdication of Emperor Francis II in 1806.

The Second Reich began in 1870 with the unification of Germany after the Franco-Prussian War and the rule of Wilhelm I. It ended with Germany's defeat in World War I and the abdication of Wilhelm II. Now, the Third Reich would revive the glory of the first two and, believed Hitler, far surpass them. The essence of Nazi ideology was, therefore, based on a combination of racism and nationalism.

In 1923, after more than three years of openly railing against the failures of the Weimar government, Hitler and six hundred of his supporters turned their ideas into bold action. Armed with machine guns, they stormed a tavern in Munich in an attempt to take control of the republic. Yet the coup quickly devolved into confusion and gunfire. The Beer Hall Putsch, as it came to be known, resulted in the deaths of sixteen Nazi Party supporters and four Bavarian police officers. The trial that followed and Hitler's fiery testimony on the stand made him a national celebrity and a favorite of the presiding judge. Despite a five-year prison sentence, Hitler was released after only eight months. The young leader used his time in jail to put his ideas of Nationalist Socialism to paper. Upon its publication in 1925, Hitler's treatise *Mein Kampf* [*My Struggle*] sold poorly. But as Hitler's popularity grew, the book came to be seen as a virtual master plan for the annihilation of the Jewish people.

Like many Europeans of his generation, Hitler grew up feeling threatened by Jews: They did not look like other Germans, they dressed differently, and their ways of worship seemed strange. Throughout the 1920s and early 1930s, Hitler built a controversial political career by exploiting these knee-jerk suspicions of all things Jewish. Although Hitler's Nazi Party promised the people of Germany economic stability and a renewed sense of purpose, his fiery speeches before ever-growing crowds also stoked the flames of German nationalism and dripped with contempt for Communists and Jews.

Journalist Ron Rosenbaum is convinced that the ancient story of Judas betraying Jesus Christ was an unofficial but potent comparison for many of the defeated Germans, including future chancellor Adolf Hitler. "Indeed," writes Rosenbaum, "one can hear incendiary anti-Semitic echoes of the Judas story in

Hitler was given a five-year prison sentence after his participation in the Beer Hall Putsch, but he was released after only eight months.

the stab-in-the-back accusation Hitler manipulated to convince the German public that the heroic German army had not lost the First World War but had been betrayed, stabbed in the back, by treacherous Jews and Jewish-paid politicians on the home front."[7]

Author Yehuda Bauer notes the willingness of the German people to go along with the anti-Semitism promoted by Hitler's National Socialist Party:

Those who voted for the Nazis knew they were voting for an anti-Semitic party, but clearly, anti-Semitism was not foremost in the minds of voters. Nor did the Nazis put anti-Semitism first among the topics that their propaganda dealt with. . . . Their campaign dealt with mass unemployment, the economic and social crisis generally, and the defeat of Germany in World War I and the consequent military and political humiliation from which Germany should rise."[8]

Taking Charge

Hitler's rise to the chancellorship of the Weimar Republic in early 1933 was viewed by many Germans as a national rebirth. Germans now had something—and someone—to believe in. Hitler promised to protect and defend the German people from invasion; he promised to rebuild the nation's economy and put citizens to work; and he promised to destroy all enemies of the state.

Now, with a mandate from the German people, he was intent on carrying those principles out. Upon his swearing in as chancellor, Hitler quickly consolidated power in line with his aim of putting all aspects of German society—politics, culture, education, the economy, the press, and more—under the control of the Nazi Party and stamping out all resistance.

In March 1933, two months after Hitler assumed the chancellorship of Germany, the first Nazi concentration camp opened in Dachau, near Munich. Its early prisoners were mostly political opponents of the new regime, but as the march to the nation's renewal began, Germany's Jewish citizens had everything to fear.

Jude

With his party now in control of the country's newspapers and radio outlets, Hitler's message of reunifying the German nation, torn apart by World War I, struck a chord with many Germans. Otto Dietrich, reich press chief, led the charge "to enrage Germans against the Jews," according to the court transcripts of a post–World War II trial, "to justify the measures taken and to be taken against them, and to subdue any doubts which might arise as to the justice of measures of racial persecution to which Jews were to be subjected."[9]

Founded on the premise that Germanic blood and Jewish blood were fundamentally different, the Nazi Party devised a plan to alienate an entire people. This plan—called Aryanization—was designed to repress Jews both socially and

Hitler's "Struggle"

In early November 1923 Adolf Hitler and his growing Nazi Party tried to overthrow the German government. The coup failed, and the World War I veteran was arrested and found guilty of high treason. Sentenced to five years in prison, Hitler began dictating his thoughts on violence, race, and politics to two associates. After his early release on December 20, 1924, the young and fiery politician continued the work. The resulting book—originally titled *Four and a Half Years of Fighting Against Lies, Stupidity, and Cowardice*—became *Mein Kampf* (*My Struggle*) and appeared in the summer of 1925. With a run of only five hundred copies, the book failed to arouse much interest with readers. But when the Nazis came to power eight years later, *Mein Kampf* struck a chord and inflamed hatred toward Hitler's twin obsessions: communism and Jewry. From the rubble of a ruined and humiliated Germany, the future

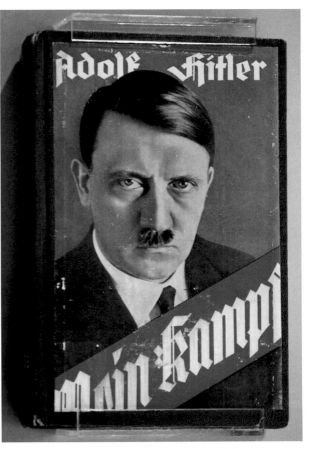

Adolf Hitler began writing Mein Kampf (My Struggle) *while he was in prison. It was published in the summer of 1925.*

chancellor laid the foundation for his ultimate plan. Years before the Holocaust began, its spiritual mastermind had already sighted his target: "If we pass all the causes of the German collapse in review, the ultimate and most decisive remains the failure to recognize the racial problem and especially the Jewish menace."

Adolf Hitler, *Mein Kampf*. www.hitler.org/writings/Mein_Kampf/mkv1ch11.html.

Nazi soldiers hold anti-Semitic placards in front of a locked storefront in the organized boycott of German Jewish businesses in 1933. The large sign reads: "Germans Defend Yourselves! Don't buy from the Jews!"

economically. On April 1, 1933, the Nazis began a boycott of Jewish-owned businesses. Carrying signs reading "The Jews Are Our Misfortune" and "Don't Buy from Jews," Hitler's brown-shirted paramilitary group, an armed force known as the SA, or Storm Troopers, scrawled *Jude* (Jew) and yellow and black Stars of David across shop doors and windows. Jewish people were beaten and taunted. A week later the new government put race laws in place that segregated and discriminated against Jewish citizens. Many literally saw the writing on the wall. In 1933 more than thirty thousand Jews emigrated from Germany. Others—either too poor to relocate or hopeful that things would improve—stayed. Germany was their home, after all.

Bad to Worse

By 1934 the situation had only worsened. Now, after purging his enemies within the government, Hitler became *Führer*, commander of both the political and military wings of the German Reich. With his new dictatorial powers, and 90 percent of the 45.5 million voting Germans behind him, he escalated his policies against the Jews.

In 1935 the party enacted the Nuremberg Laws, one of which distinguished between "citizens" and "subjects." The former included only those of "German or related blood."[10] Jews, excluded from this group, were henceforth categorized as "subjects" who were not entitled to the benefits of citizenship. This idea of racial purity soon became a hallmark of prejudice against Jews. Stripped of their citizenship, Jews were subjected to more acts of blatant anti-Semitism. Marriage between Jews and non-Jews was forbidden; Jewish university professors were fired from their jobs; patronizing Jewish-owned businesses was banned; and Jews could no longer "employ in their households female subjects of German or kindred blood who were under 45 years old."[11] This racist fear among some Germans that Jewish men might corrupt

young Aryan females was promoted in Nazi propaganda. The stereotype of the sexually charged Semite became a fixture in the war on German Jews.

Other racist Jewish stereotypes such as long, crooked noses, wide mouths, and a lust for money took hold in the minds of many Germans during this time. These notions, combined with the legal definition of what a Jew was, became an obsession in the new Germany. Doctors measured a person's features with sharp metal instruments, and one's ancestry became of utmost importance. People flooded church registries and sought out birth certificates to determine how much, if any, Jewish blood ran through their veins.

Such hysteria even found its way into children's books. One example from a 1936 publication read in part, "The Devil is the father of the Jew. When God created the world, He invented the races: The Indians, the Negroes, the Chinese, And also the wicked creature called the Jew."[12]

Kristallnacht

A turning point in the Nazis' war against the Jews occurred in Paris, France, on November 3, 1938. That day, seventeen-year-old Polish Jew Herschel Grynszpan received a desperate letter from his sister Berta in Germany: The Grynszpan family was being deported back to Poland under direct orders from the Nazi regime. Quick-tempered and impulsive, Herschel Grynszpan fretted about what to do. For twenty years his family had struggled to survive in the German city

Anti-Semitism: "Revolt Against Humanity"

Anti-Semitism, the hatred of people of Jewish origin, began during the days of early Christianity. The consensus among early Christians was that Jews had killed Jesus, their savior. In the first century, a Greek philosopher echoed this sentiment when he wrote that "Jews have long been in . . . revolt against humanity." Later, during the Crusades, as European armies attempted to reclaim the Holy Land from Islam, anti-Jewish demonstrations and targeted killing of Jews and the burning of synagogues were common. In the Middle Ages Jews were expelled from Spain, England, and France, or suffered forced conversion to Christianity. The Spanish Inquisition, which began in 1478 and lasted, officially, until 1834, tortured Jews and put them to death unless they relinquished their long-held beliefs and traditions. Many inquisitors were later canonized as saints in the Roman Catholic Church. Medieval superstitions and rumors—Jews had sharp teeth, horns, and special powers—kept otherwise peaceful people in fear of Jews. In modern times the stereotypes spread, condemning Jews as greedy, sexually deviant, untrustworthy, and cowardly. Despite the founding of the state of Israel in 1948 and the wider acceptance of Jews around the world, anti-Semitism remains a threat to civilized societies.

of Hanover. Now they were being thrown out.

Three days after receiving the letter, Grynszpan left his apartment. He checked into the Hotel de Suez and stayed the night. After breakfast on the morning of November 7, he made his way to a gun shop named the Sharp Blade in the Saint Martin district of Paris and purchased a pistol. "Why do you need the gun?" the shop owner asked. "I am a foreigner," Grynszpan told him, "and I have to carry large amounts of money for my father."[13]

Soon after, Grynszpan took a train to the German embassy and asked to see third secretary Ernst von Rath. He had a message for him, he said. After being ushered into the secretary's office, Grynszpan pulled his gun from his pocket and fired five times at von Rath. Von Rath died two days later. When asked about his crime of revenge against Germany for its treatment of its Jews, Grynszpan said, "To be Jewish is not a crime. We are not animals. The Jewish people have a right to live."[14]

News of the assassination spread quickly. The German, Nazi-controlled press, in particular, made sure its readers knew that a Jew was responsible. The murder of a Nazi official by a Jew became the excuse to unleash more hatred and violence on the entire Jewish population.

As evening turned into darkest night, and night turned into morning, the skies all across Germany and Austria were set ablaze by soldiers and people on the streets. In the event known as *Kristallnacht*, or "Night of Broken Glass," seventy-five hundred Jewish-owned businesses had their windows smashed, a thousand synagogues were burned, cemeteries were desecrated, and Jewish citizens were dragged from their houses and beaten. Four hundred of them died. In most places, firefighters stood watching, told only to stop the flames from spreading to other, non-Jewish areas.

Johanna Gerechter Neumann was a young girl in Hamburg, Germany, and remembers the utter destruction she witnessed that night: "What we saw was hordes of people standing in front of a beautiful synagogue, and throwing stones through these magnificent, uh, colored windows. And, uh, as we arrived, of course we ran past the, the, the place itself, the noise, the shouting, the screaming."[15]

On January 25, 1939, German foreign minister Joachim von Ribbentrop would distribute a circular that contained what was perhaps the most direct evidence yet about what the Nazis had in store for Europe's Jewish populace: "It is not by chance that 1938, the year of our destiny, saw the realization of our plan for Greater Germany as well as a major step towards the solution of the Jewish problem."[16]

The March to War

The Third Reich wanted to go to war to increase the size of Germany. This militarism and territorial expansion was justified under the banner of *lebensraum*, or "living space," which Hitler portrayed as Germany's destiny. Hitler's regime also claimed the right to reclaim territory that rightfully belonged to the German people, taken from them under the terms of the Treaty of Versailles.

On March 12, 1938, Germany took an important, aggressive step by sending troops across the border into Austria, incorporating the neighboring country in an operation known as the *Anschluss*, or "link-up." Hitler desired to do the same with much of eastern Europe. As he strengthened his army in violation of the treaty, Hitler and Soviet dictator Joseph Stalin signed the German-Soviet Pact in August 1939. This planned ten-year agreement stipulated that the two countries would not attack one another. It also contained a secret protocol that divided Poland and the rest of eastern Europe into German and Soviet areas. The pact became the first step toward a proposed domination of all of Europe by the two powers.

Other European nations, including Great Britain, at first refused to believe the rumors of an agreement between the two bitter enemies. British prime minister Neville Chamberlain told his Cabinet only a month before that he "could not bring himself to believe that a real alliance between Germany and the Soviet Union was possible."[17] Hitler wasted little time in proving Chamberlain wrong.

On September 1, 1939, Germany invaded Poland, claiming it as part of Greater Germany. This "September Campaign," as many Poles referred to it, began with the German air force's bombing of the city of Wielun. But it did not stop there. By land, by sea, and through the air, German forces pounded Polish towns and military installations, creating chaos and exerting control.

During the first night of the invasion, William Luksenburg watched as one of his neighbors disobeyed curfew and tried to cross the street. After a German soldier yelled for him to stop, the neighbor boy began running. The German soldier fired on the child, who fell down dead in front of the Luksenburg house. The soldiers ordered Luksenburg and others to carry the body away. When he got home afterward, he was drenched with blood: "I will always remember my mother's . . . expression and my mother's fear and my mother's cry out when she saw me completely covered with blood and that was the first night. . . . We didn't know what's coming and it was a horrible thing, that first night."[18] With the aid of its new, and temporary, ally the Soviet Union, the Nazis overran Poland in little more than a month.

Germany's invasion of Poland prompted declarations of war from Great

Adolf Hitler and other top German officers watch Nazi soldiers march through the mud of Poland after Germany attacked Poland in the morning hours of September 1, 1939.

Britain, Australia, and New Zealand. The German people began enlisting in the army in droves. For some, this new war was an echo of the old one—the one which had resulted in defeat and economic collapse and dishonor. Yet scholar Niall Ferguson draws a distinction between the First and Second World Wars: "Strategically, though, the idea that in some way the Second World War is the First World War all over again is, I think, wrong because Hitler quite clearly saw the need to learn lessons from the mistakes of 1914."[19]

One of those lessons, as Hitler saw it, was to wipe out one's enemies with no mercy and no remorse. Earlier that year Hitler connected a future war to the fate of the Jews. In a speech at the Reichstag, or Parliament, he made himself clearer than ever before: "I want today to be a prophet again: if international finance and Jewry inside and outside Europe should succeed in plunging the nations once more into a world war, the result will be not . . . the victory of Jewry, but the annihilation of the Jewish race in Europe."[20]

By 1939 the German Jewish population had dwindled. Many had fled the Third Reich's racial laws, blatant prejudice, and growing violence against Jews. Many others had been imprisoned. Now, the invasion of Poland presented the Nazis with both a challenge and an opportunity. The regime controlled a Polish Jewish population of nearly 3 million. As de facto rulers of a new nation, German financial and military resources would be stretched to their limits. Yet if a plan could be devised to deal with the massive number of Polish Jews, the Nazis' goal of a Jew-free Europe might someday become a reality.

Chapter Two

From Barracks to Death Camp

Europe was now at war, and Hitler's armies went on a campaign of conquest that seemed unstoppable. Over the next two years, the Nazis would seize control of territory where the vast majority of Europe's Jews lived. Hitler's answer to the question of what to do with the Jews in the occupied lands and with massive numbers of prisoners of war would eventually center on, among other places, the small Polish district town of Oświęcim, which the Germans translated as Auschwitz. But in the early days of the war, the Nazis' efforts centered on containment of Jews rather than their extermination.

Jewish Ghettos

Heinrich Himmler, Hitler's second in command, was a bespectacled and ruthless Nazi commander obsessed with racial purity. He longed to weed out non-Aryans from the ranks of the German people he claimed to serve. As he built his police forces in the years leading up to the Second World War, his perfect specimens had to meet certain requirements: They had to be at least five feet eight (173cm) in height and be able to trace their racially pure Germanic ancestry back to at least 1800—1750 for officers. "Himmler's ideal," writes historian Klaus P. Fischer, "was a racial utopia dominated by new Aryan God-men who would redeem Germany from its suffering and evil."[21]

But to create such an ideal state, those deemed of impure blood would have to be gotten rid of. Himmler, therefore, was always looking for more effective and more impersonal methods of doing away with Jews. Initially, deportation, perhaps to Africa, seemed like a good plan. But transporting millions of people to another, far-off continent quickly proved impractical for the Nazis. The answer to their Jewish problem eventually came from another Nazi official, SS lieutenant

No Escape

Between 1933 and 1940, more than four hundred thousand Jews left Germany behind. What began as a trickle became a flood by early 1939. As the Third Reich imposed stiffer laws that stripped Jews of their remaining rights, some families escaped east to Poland; others, if they could afford it, moved to Great Britain, the United States, or Canada. By September 1939 passage out of Germany had become virtually impossible. There, as well as in Poland, Czechoslovakia, and Austria, Jews were forced to wear yellow Stars of David and carry identification cards wherever they went. Men and women were often dragged from their houses and beaten, or lined up against a wall with a dozen others and mowed down by machine gun fire. Each day brought only more fear and heartache as the Nazi menace descended across eastern Europe. Many families wiled away the hours huddled in their homes, awaiting the inevitable knock on the door. When it came, Nazi soldiers ordered them into the streets and led them to holding camps or trains heading east. Most would never see their houses or streets again.

colonel Adolf Eichmann, who devised the idea of confining Jews to massive European ghettos. Since Jews would not simply disappear, Eichmann, Himmler, and Hitler soon came to believe that they could at least be kept separate from the purer Aryan population.

Less than four months after Germany's invasion of Poland, the first large-scale Jewish ghetto was established in the Polish city of Tuliszkow. Ghettos in Lodz and Warsaw soon followed. The ghettos—ramshackle tenement buildings with no heat and little drinking water—were walled off from the rest of the city in which they were located. Jews trying to escape were typically shot. Warsaw held the largest of these cramped and dirty places, eventually housing 380,000 people in an area that accounted for barely 2.5 percent of the entire city.

Life in the ghetto was a daily struggle to survive. Food was scarce and sanitation nearly nonexistent. Garbage was everywhere.

Emmanuel Ringelblum learned the horrors firsthand while living in the Warsaw ghetto. For him the worst part of the experience was seeing children freezing in the wintertime: "They whine, beg, sing, lament and tremble in the cold," Ringelblum wrote in his diary, "without underwear, without clothes, without shoes, covered only by rags and bags which are tied by strings to meager skeletons."[22]

Nazi leaders viewed the ghettos as the first step on the road toward Jewish eradication. Before long, as overcrowding resulted in starvation and death, they devised even more reliable methods of destruction.

A little more than a year after the first Nazi-controlled ghetto was established in Tuliszkow, a document prepared for Himmler circulated among Nazi officials. The document, distributed on December 4, 1940, contained statistics on the number of Jews remaining in the German Reich. The report's title, "The Final Solution of the Jewish Question," suggested transferring "the Jews out of the European economic space of the German people to a still-to-be-determined territory."[23] Such a plan would involve the deportation of millions.

Nazi SS soldiers line up and shoot Jews before pushing them into a trench that already contains the bodies of victims.

Murder in the East

Jewish ghettos were only part of the plan for the Jews of Europe. Soon after Poland fell, the Nazis sent out their most loyal guard—a paramilitary police force of some 240,000 men known as *Schutzstaffel*, or SS—to root out and destroy all enemies of the German state. The SS was originally a small force that served as Hitler's personal bodyguard—now, under the leadership of Heinrich Himmler, SS units became the administrators of the occupied territories and Hitler's network of concentration and labor camps. They had free rein to persecute and brutalize those of Jewish descent, prisoners of war, and any individuals bold enough to disagree with the Third Reich's policies. These death squads murdered over fifteen thousand Poles.

Additional mobile killing units called *Einsatzgruppen* were activated to follow the German armies on the eastern front and kill saboteurs, Jews, and Communists. Divided into four battalion-size groups labeled A through D, the Einsatzgruppen conducted a reign of terror that many historians view as the forerunner of, and parallel to, the systematic murder of innocent civilians that would soon be institutionalized in the death camps.

Some Nazi commanders hesitated to kill civilians, not because they felt the murder of innocents was wrong, but because they were not sure their men could carry out such orders and not be physically sickened. Soldiers are trained to gaze down the barrel of their rifles and shoot armed enemies. This would be different: Their victims would carry no weapons and pose no physical threat. They were marked for death only because the Nazi state said so.

Einsatzgruppen officers, therefore, often prepared their men through a "stepwise escalation of the killing," says scholar Daniel Jonah Goldhagen. "First, by shooting primarily teenage and adult Jewish males, they would be able to acclimate themselves to mass executions without the shock of killing women, young children, and the infirm."[24]

In their roundups, German officers and soldiers took advantage of the anti-Semitism long entrenched in small villages across eastern Europe. With the help of local Ukrainian, Latvian, and Lithuanian informants, Einsatzgruppen identified the Jews and Gypsies, or Rom, another undesirable ethnic group, in an occupied area. Houses were attacked, and victims were dragged into the streets, then marched or driven to execution sites, usually simple ravines or fields into which long trenches had already been dug. Sometimes the terrified victims were forced at gunpoint to dig the holes themselves. All were ordered to hand over any rings, bracelets, watches, wallets, and money—anything of value—and remove their clothes. Frima Laub remembers what happened next: "The women remained with the underwear only, and the men in their shorts. My mother wasn't fast enough to take off her gold earrings so she was hit by a Gestapo

Nazi Euthanasia

Aktion T4, the Nazi euthanasia program, began in the fall of 1939. As Hitler's army poured into Poland, medical staff at six centers checked medical records and decided who would live and who would die. Doctors, nurses, and midwives were under orders to register children up to three years of age who appeared mentally retarded, physically deformed, or unusual in any other way. A questionnaire, distributed to those who treated the patient, had to be filled out. Then, medical staff, many of whom had not examined the children themselves, made a decision for or against what Hitler called a "mercy death." A red plus sign indicated a serious defect in the child and a recommendation to kill him or her; a blue minus sign meant the child was to live. Three plus signs meant certain death. Before long the program was expanded to include older children, adults, and those suffering from such mental disorders as schizophrenia. The German psychiatric clinic Hadamar became infamous, in large part because of the merciless tactics of its director Christian Wirth, known to inmates and SS alike by the ironic nickname the "savage Christian." The euthanasia program became a proving ground for the gas chambers used by the Nazis later in the war. At least one hundred thousand people had died by the time the program ceased.

Quoted in *The History Place*, "Nazi Euthanasia." www.historyplace.com/worldwar2/holocaust/h-euthanasia.htm.

with . . . the handle of a rifle. And . . . she fell down. We picked her up."[25]

Laub, her mother, and her sister survived the ordeal by pretending not to be Jewish, but such tricks rarely worked. Instead, villagers were ordered from their homes and forced to march to central locations where they were told to undress and line up in front of long trenches or in the trenches themselves. Seconds later, these naked, frightened villagers were mowed down by machine gun fire. Bulldozers or men with shovels filled in the trenches.

The murderers themselves, many no older than eighteen or twenty, responded in various ways to their morbid task. Hans Friedrich, a member of an SS infantry unit supporting the Einsatzgruppen in the Ukraine, says his unit experienced little or no resistance from the victims: "They [the Jews] were extremely shocked, utterly frightened and petrified, and you could do what you wanted with them."[26] Friedrich willingly admits to shooting Jews, Gypsies, and others. When asked what went through his mind as he looked down

Heinrich Himmler took a lead role in the extermination of Jews.

the barrel of his rifle at naked men, women, and children preparing to die, he says, "I only thought, 'Aim carefully so that you hit.' When you've got to the point where you're standing there with a gun ready to shoot . . . there's only one thing, a calm hand so that you hit well. Nothing else."[27] Although more than a million Jews and tens of thousands of Gypsies, Communist officials, and disabled people died at the hands of the Einsatzgruppen, Friedrich claimed to feel no sense of remorse. Nor, he said, had he lost one night of sleep thinking about it.

Oświęcim: From Town to Prison Camp

As the mass slaughter in the east continued, the Third Reich also increased the number of concentration camps, which soon dotted the occupied territories of Greater Germany. Many within Germany had already been in operation for eight years. But with Third Reich forces pushing deeper into Soviet territory, more room for political enemies would be needed. So it happened that the Nazi leadership decided to create a new forced labor camp near a small town in the Upper Silesia region of southwestern Poland.

Considered unsuitable as living space for German citizens because of its barrenness and damp climate, the area near the village of Oświęcim seemed the perfect place for a holding camp—a place in which prisoners would be temporarily kept until being moved to other camps. But soon after discovering the spot, Nazi officials made the camp permanent. They

also translated the Polish "Oświęcim" into the German "Auschwitz."

On April, 30, 1940, thirty-nine-year-old SS captain Rudolf Höss was made the camp's first commandant. Originally conceived of as a concentration camp like Dachau, Auschwitz borrowed the procedures and dehumanizing tactics that had been effective at Dachau, Höss's previous post. Theodor Eicke, Dachau's first commandant, specialized in ordered brutality—including beatings and torture. While the average stay for prisoners lasted about a year, Eicke and other officials could shorten or lengthen the sentence at will. Despite the torturous uncertainty, thousands did eventually leave.

Another system introduced by Eicke at Dachau consisted of "Kapos." Probably derived from the Italian word "capo" or "head," camp officers chose a prisoner to lead the separate blocks, or areas of the camp. Kapos, in an effort to impress their jailers, could often be crueler than the Nazis themselves. And if they failed to do their jobs, they could quickly be sent back to live with the other inmates—a fate that would mean certain death.

In Dachau the Nazis first tried to process and manage large groups of people. They also put into practice chilling ethics, demanding loyalty, unquestioning obedience, and hardness from the guards. Eicke demanded such things, and more: "Anyone who shows even the slightest vestige of sympathy towards them [prisoners] must immediately vanish from our ranks. I need only hard, totally committed SS men. There is no place amongst us for soft people."[28]

Auschwitz's first inmates were thirty German criminals transferred from Sachsenhausen concentration camp in northern Germany. They were quickly made Kapos to help control those who came after them. A trainload of mostly Polish university students—rounded up for being subversive—were the first to feel the Kapos' wrath. One of the new arrivals, Wilhelm Brasse, remembers helping build the camp: "We used very primitive tools. The prisoners had to carry stones. It was very difficult, hard labor. And we were beaten."[29]

According to Brasse, the Kapos were encouraged by German soldiers to punish the other prisoners harshly. In return for their cruelty, the Kapos were rewarded with cigarettes or soup. Under such circumstances, the Polish prisoners quickly learned that certain Kapos were better to work for than others. In short order, Rudolf Höss was ordered to increase the camp's capacity for inmates. His superior, SS commander Oswald Pohl, also suggested Höss integrate the camp into the Reich-owned German Earth and Stone Works as a way of financially supporting itself and Greater Germany.

For his part, Höss had learned from his own time in prison that work is what keeps a prisoner alive and helps him or her face the new day while behind bars. Not long after taking command, Höss ordered prisoners to post a message that would become an ironic symbol of the brutality and disguised purpose of Auschwitz. In letters bent out of wrought iron above the camp gate, the sign read: "Arbeit macht frei" (Work brings freedom).

Wannsee

In December 1941, fourteen German state secretaries and other high-ranking officials met at a lavish guesthouse on 56-58 Strasse Am Grossen Wannsee. This secret gathering, now known as the Wannsee Conference, was led by Reinhard Heydrich, chief of the Main Office for the Security of the Reich. After the Nazi officials took time to chat and enjoy refreshments, Heydrich rose to speak. According to minutes taken at the meeting, Heydrich first announced to all in attendance that he had been appointed to lead preparations for the "final solution."

Historian Saul Friedländer writes that Heydrich then "presented a brief historical survey of the measures already taken to segregate the Jews of the Reich and force them to emigrate. After further emigration had been forbidden in October 1941 . . . another solution had been authorized by the Führer: the evacuation of the Jews of Europe to the East."[30]

Heydrich now listed the Jews to be targeted, country by country. He spoke of healthy Jews versus older or infirm Jews. He talked of an "evacuation . . . to the East," after which individuals would be divided by sex as well as by their ability to work building roads. "The Jews will be conscripted for labor," said Heydrich, "and undoubtedly a large number of them will drop out through natural wastage."[31]

Hungry and dirty children gather in the Jewish Warsaw ghetto. Survival was difficult in the Warsaw ghetto where food was scarce and sanitation was virtually nonexistent.

Despite the hard labor that awaited many of the Nazi's prisoners, one of Heydrich's chief concerns was that large numbers of them might survive the Third Reich's attempt to work them to death. According to historian Laurence Rees, "These were the very Jews that natural selection would have determined were the most dangerous to the Nazis. These Jews, said Heydrich, must also be 'treated accordingly.'"[32]

Heydrich's fourteen colleagues, eight of whom held academic doctorates, did not need to hear the words to know what Heydrich and his absent superiors now proposed for Europe's Jewish population: extermination.

After the main presentation, the Nazi officials discussed the legal definition of "Jew." What, exactly, constituted "Jewishness"—a father, a mother, a grandparent with Semitic blood? Could

The wrought iron message over the camp gate at Auschwitz reads "work brings freedom."

such people be sterilized, deported, or both? Might "half Jews" be sent to special labor camps set up for others like them? Few firm conclusions were reached, and historians continue to debate the importance of the Wannsee Conference, but the meeting did make one thing absolutely clear: The plan for the "Final Solution" was now in place.

Expansion of the Jewish Population Under German Control

Himmler's challenge was clear: what to do with all of the Polish Jews under Nazi control? By 1940, with dozens of ghettos already overcrowded and difficult to manage, Reichsführer SS Himmler looked for other options for the Jews of Poland and other eastern European conquered territory.

He had already ordered soldiers to begin killing women and children during Einsatzgruppen raids in the east. Himmler even added forty thousand more soldiers to the death squads for the purpose of speeding up the process. Another method, too, looked promising. Germany's Criminal Technical Institute had developed a process by which up to forty Soviets or Poles could be placed in a sealed van. A metal pipe connected to the exhaust gas hose then pumped carbon monoxide back into the van, killing the people inside in a matter of minutes. One commando remembered "the hammering [to escape] and the screaming of the Jews" and how "As the doors were opened dense smoke emerged, followed by a tangle of crumpled bodies."[33] Within months, thirty such gas vans traveled across the Baltic countries, Serbia, and Belorussia.

The Einsatzgruppen's operations expanded greatly beginning in June 1941, when Germany invaded its former ally, the Soviet Union, at that time home to some 5 million Jews. Betrayed by Hitler, Stalin declared war on Germany and its allies and joined the Allies by fighting German armies on a new, huge, eastern front.

The First Mass Gas Chambers

In planning the invasion of Russia, known as Operation Barbarossa, Heydrich ordered all Jews killed regardless of age or gender. But with additional millions of Jews as well as thousands of Soviet prisoners of war to do away with, small-scale extermination methods such as gassing vans and mass shootings would no longer suffice. Gas chambers made to look like showers were built in a small number of concentration camps that would be known as the death camps, because their primary purpose was the systemized extermination of people sent there.

The first gas chambers were tested at Chelmno, which opened in December 1941. Other killing centers followed, including Treblinka, Belzec, and Sobibor. For racially obsessed groups like the Nazis and their followers, the murder of handicapped people made perfect sense. One doctor in the euthanasia program described his feelings on the matter this way: "The idea is unbearable to me that the best, the flower of our youth must lose its life at the front, in order that the feeble-minded and irresponsible asocial elements can have a secure existence in the asylum."[34]

The euthanasia program—known as 14f13—came to Auschwitz on July 28, 1941. Prisoners were told at evening roll call that the sick could leave and be made well again. While some inmates did not believe it, five hundred others either chose to leave or were chosen by guards. They were taken to a waiting train, transported to a mental hospital near Danzig, and gassed. This was the first time at Auschwitz that the Nazis had used poison to kill prisoners they deemed unfit to work. It would not be the last.

Deadly Breakthrough

In time, this method of destruction would be used on perfectly healthy individuals considered unable to work or simply useless. Scholars disagree about exactly when gassing at Auschwitz became common practice for larger groups of prisoners. What is clear is that a technological breakthrough occurred in the summer of 1941.

These empty Zyklon B gas containers held the poison used to kill millions of concentration camp prisoners.

The euthanasia program doctors typically used carbon monoxide to kill their patients. But delivery to Auschwitz from Berlin would be time-consuming and costly. Knowing this, Karl Fritzsch, Höss's deputy, had the idea of using a different chemical cocktail, one that was readily available and in great abundance.

Auschwitz had been built from the run-down and abandoned barracks of the Polish army. The barracks, crawling with lice, rats, and cockroaches, needed fumigation. For that purpose camp guards used prussic acid, or cyanide, which came in cans and was sold under the label Zyklon (cyclone) Blausäure (cyanide). Zyklon B, Fritzsch and Höss came to believe, could be used on human cockroaches. Now Höss had only to decide on a place to test the product.

As Auschwitz became a fully functioning camp in late 1940 and early 1941, few buildings were as frightening to inmates as Block 11. Part of the original camp building and built from red brick, Block 11 was unexceptional to look at. But word quickly spread that it was where prisoners went to be tortured and killed. For Höss it appeared to be the perfect place to test this newly discovered method of mass slaughter.

As the SS men worked to prepare the building, many prisoners understood the hubbub was meant for them. "I could see that they were bringing in soil in wheelbarrows to insulate the windows," says Brasse. "And one day I saw them take the severely sick out on stretchers from the hospital and they were taken to Block 11."[35] Along with ill prisoners, the Nazis experimented on Russian officers. In one instance the gas failed to work completely, and some of the Russians were left alive, only to die another day. Höss himself witnessed at least one gassing in Block 11 and later detailed the event: "Protected by a gas mask, I watched the killing myself. In the crowded cells death came instantaneously the moment the Zyklon B was thrown in. A short, almost smothered cry and it was all over."[36]

Auschwitz II: Birkenau

As Germany's remaining Jews were branded with yellow stars of identification and whispering about the fate of so many others in the east, the Third Reich had a new plan for Auschwitz: expansion. Himmler visited Auschwitz for the first time in March 1941 and told Höss the camp would be expanded from ten thousand prisoners to thirty thousand. Thus, more room would be needed. Officially designated as Auschwitz II, Brzezinka, or Birkenau in German, stood almost 2 miles (3km) from the main camp. Intended for prisoners of war, the village of Birkenau was cleared in the summer and fall of 1941, its Polish inhabitants relocated.

According to the original design, Birkenau's barracks would each contain 550 inmates, but this already high number was upped to 744. The Nazi leadership saw nothing wrong with such a plan, since most of the men that would fill Birkenau were Russian prisoners of war. Aside from the Jews, the Russians,

Lifeline: Irena Sendler

Each day during the Second World War, Irena Sendler risked her life. After the Nazis invaded Poland on September 1, 1939—the start of World War II in Europe—Sendler created Zegota, an underground group founded to save children from the Warsaw ghetto in Poland. A Roman Catholic by faith, Sendler and her volunteers did whatever they had to in order to smuggle the youngest and most fragile of the Polish Jews to safety: Children were placed in coffins and ambulances—anything to ferry them from certain death. At times, Jewish children were sent into church confessionals and given papers making them "Catholic." They would then be adopted by a Christian home or sent to an orphanage or convent. In 2007, after being honored by the Polish government, Sendler wrote, "Every child saved with my help and the help of all the wonderful secret messengers . . . is the justification of my existence on this earth, and not a title to glory." Generations survive because of her efforts. Irena Sendler died in May 2008 at the age of ninety-eight.

Quoted in Dennis Hevesi, "Irena Sendler, Lifeline to Young Jews, Is Dead at 98," *New York Times*, May 13, 2008. www.nytimes.com/2008/05/13/world/europe/13sendler.html.

as Communists, remained the most hated Nazi enemy.

The Soviet POWs helped build the new facility. More than ten thousand began the massive project in the fall; only a few hundred survived into the spring. The life expectancy in the early days of Birkenau was two weeks. Survivors speak of unimaginable Nazi brutality—beatings, torture, and starvation—that before long turned them against one another. In at least one case, desperately hungry prisoners even resorted to cannibalism. "I myself came across a Russian," wrote Höss in his diary, "lying between piles of bricks, whose body had been torn open and the liver removed. They would beat each other to death for food."[37] Ironically, for Höss and other SS, this simply reinforced their long-held belief that their prisoners were subhuman and did not deserve better treatment. SS member Perry Broad recalls Birkenau as a much harsher place than Auschwitz I, the main camp. According to Broad, the ground always seemed damp and basic conditions needed for human survival remained absent. "Feet drop into a sticky bog at every step," said Broad, "There was hardly any water for washing."[38]

The Nazis divided Birkenau into at least a dozen sections, separating them from each other by electrified barbed wire. Women stayed in one area, men in another. There was also a family camp for Rom, or Gypsies, where relatives could live together. This portion of Auschwitz-Birkenau became one of the most disease-ridden, with a constantly high death rate from ailments such as smallpox and dysentery. By January 1942 the death rate from disease and starvation had sharply increased at Auschwitz, although the gassing experiments of Block 11 had yet to become a systematic method of destruction. This soon changed. Auschwitz's days as a notorious death camp had only just begun.

Chapter Three

Factory of Death

The Third Reich took more than a decade to perfect their methods of destroying members of the human race. Through conditioned obedience and commitment to the Aryan ideal, members of the Nazi Party created a system designed to manufacture death in the most streamlined and efficient way possible, either through bone-crushing, back-breaking labor or immediate mass execution. Auschwitz is best understood through the stories of those who survived—and those who did not. For most of them the journey began at home.

Deportation

For those Jews remaining in countries such as Germany, Poland, or Hungary, escape was no longer an option. Already herded into ghettos with little food and running water, many families—desperate and weary—could do nothing to change their fates. SS officials often demanded that local Jewish councils pro-duce lists of people for deportation. Letters then went out ordering those listed to report to deportation centers. The Nazis did not reveal destinations, only saying that the Jews were being relocated to work farms in the east. Later, in an effort to speed up the process, SS squads were sent from house to house rounding up dozens of Jews at a time.

According to historian Daniel Jonah Goldhagen, German citizens, with a few exceptions, encouraged this mass expulsion of its remaining Jewish population. "The depth of ordinary Germans' anti-Semitic passion was such," writes Goldhagen, "that scenes of open, enthusiastic reveling in the Jews' expected fate occurred in Berlin as the Jews were assembled for deportation."[39] One German woman, appalled at such scenes, recalls people standing in doorways and shouting, "Look at the impudent Jews. Now they are still laughing, but their final short hour has rung."[40]

Jews deported from Hungary leave a German boxcar and step onto a crowded railway platform at the Auschwitz concentration camp.

Some of those detained had to wait days for transport and were kept like caged animals behind barbed wire fences in temporary camps with little to eat. Stella Marcus recalls transport selection: "We all were lined up, always at night, with our backpacks, waiting to see if we would be called. They told us, 'We are resettling you. We want all the Jews together in one place. And then you will work for us.'"[41] Although Stella and her mother managed to survive the Holocaust, the first step on their long journey was only beginning. Boxcars made for cattle awaited them and thousands of others who descended on the station platform crying in fear and trying to remain with their families.

Loading these "special" freight trains could take five or six hours. Travel time could take hours or days. The cattle cars were so jammed with people that there was nowhere to sit; they lacked food, water, and often fresh air. Many victims died standing up. Those who did survive recall the torturous ride and the desperate urge to live, even under the harshest conditions imaginable. Ruth Kluger describes a June 1944 train ride to Auschwitz this way:

The doors were sealed, and air came through a small rectangle that served as window. . . . Only one person could stand in this privileged spot, and he was not likely to give it up. . . . There were simply too many of us. . . . Soon the wagon reeked with the various smells that humans produce if they have to stay where they are. . . . It was summer, the temperature rose. The still air smelled of sweat, urine, excrement. A whiff of panic trembled in the air.[42]

At times the cars were so jammed and lacking in air that those inside suffocated before arrival at the death camps. One day Siegbert Löffler and a group of other Auschwitz prisoners were told they would be unloading furniture from arriving boxcars. After a few minutes' walk, they approached three railcars near the gates of Auschwitz. But, Löffler says, when he and the others arrived at the depot,

I knew right away we weren't unloading furniture. When the doors were opened each car contained corpses. The one I emptied had about 94 or 97. . . . And in each car there were little girls two, three, four years old, all dressed up like dolls, as if they were going to a birthday party. It made you think of your own children and want to be careful carrying them. An SS man hit me in the back with his club—I can still feel it today—until we grabbed them by their hair or their arms and tossed them out. We were told if we said anything, we would be immediately shot.[43]

Arrival and Selection

Prisoners who survived the transport arrived at Auschwitz desperate for water, weak, and frightened. Without warning, they might hear the sounds of a large gate clanging open. The train suddenly stopped and the boxcar doors flew open. Police dogs barked, people screamed. Squads of workers separated them from their luggage and other possessions, which they were told would be returned to them. The arrivals were herded along "the ramp," the long strip of pavement next to the railway where chaos was deliberately designed to intimidate the arrivals. "Everything went so fast," remembers Leo Schneiderman. "Men separated from women. Children torn from the arms of mothers. The elderly chased like cattle."[44]

Beginning in 1943, camp doctor Captain Josef Mengele stood on the ramp as transports were unloaded and paraded past him. He eyed each prisoner carefully, assessing vitality and strength, ability to work, and specific characteristics that might qualify an arrival for medical experimentation. Quickly he pointed at each person to step to the right (*rechts*, in German) or the left (*links*). His instantaneous decision meant life or death. Roughly 10 percent of new arrivals, the ones directed to step to the right—mostly men and teenage boys—were sent off to work; the other 90 percent—primarily women and children, directed to step to the left—were sent directly to the gas chambers.

If prisoners survived this test, they were formally processed in a series of

An Auschwitz survivor displays his prison number tattoo, still prominent more than sixty years after the Holocaust.

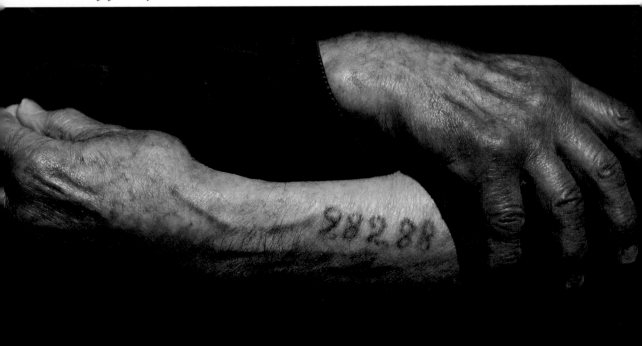

dehumanizing steps. First, they were told to strip off their clothes and put them on hooks behind them—shoes on the floor. At the next station barbers cut off all their body hair. Smaller prisoners were made to stand on stools. Once all of their hair was gone, prisoners were tattooed.

Auschwitz is the only camp that tattooed its inmates. After one person swabbed a prisoner's left forearm, the next took up a needle and inked a number on it. Clothing came next: striped brown shirt, jacket, pants, and cap; wooden clogs. Prisoners received no underwear. After receiving their clothes, they were handed two strips of cloth with the Star of David and the tattooed number on them. One was sewn onto the left breast, the other onto the right pant leg. Finally, prisoners were given a small, round bowl for daily rations. This bowl became their lifeline.

Women and men were then separately forced into disinfecting showers. Former prisoner Cecilie Klein-Pollack remembers being forced into showers soon after her arrival. Shorn of her hair

Rudolf Höss: Nazi "Grocery Clerk"

According to those who knew him, Rudolf Höss's appearance belied his capacity for mass murder. American lawyer Whitney Harris questioned Höss after the war and says the Auschwitz commander looked like "a normal person, like a grocery clerk." This impression—of a quiet man in perfect control of himself—was shared by German soldiers and camp prisoners alike. Höss considered himself an efficient, innovative bureaucrat, a normal man who valued obedience above all, and who led an otherwise uneventful life.

Höss, like Nazi leader Heinrich Himmler, grew up with a demanding father. He served in World War I as one of the youngest noncommissioned officers in the German army and, like Hitler, had been awarded the Iron Cross for bravery. After the war, he was imprisoned for five years for his right-wing political beliefs and his membership in Hitler's National Socialist Party. Upon release, Höss took up farming and joined an agricultural community called the Artamans, got married, and started a family. In 1934 Himmler—then Germany's chief of police—made Höss an enticing offer: Turn away from farming and join the Führer's personal bodyguard unit—the *Schutzstaffel*. Höss accepted and changed the course of world history.

Laurence Rees, *Auschwitz: A New History*. New York: Public Affairs, 2005, p. 2.

and frightened, she says, "They first opened the hot water, so we were scalded and as we ran out from under the hot water, we were beaten back by the SS and by the Kapos to go under the showers again, so they opened the ice cold water, which had the same effect."[45] Most were well aware of rumors that people were being gassed to death in the camps under the ruse of taking showers, which only intensified the terror of the experience.

While new arrivals were initiated into the camp system, slave laborers pored over the valuables of those just stripped of all their belongings. In Auschwitz, you lost not only your freedom, but your worldly possessions. You were now utterly at the mercy of the Third Reich.

Hard Labor

For most Auschwitz inmates, selection for work was only a temporary reprieve from death, and the kind of labor they were subjected to was often horrific. Hours were long, the work itself nearly unbearable. This "annihilation through labor" destroyed the bodies and the will of hundreds of thousands of camp prisoners. Forced to subsist on meager rations and little water, if a prisoner broke down or was unable to work, the SS guard, keeping an eye out, sent him to the gas chambers. Auschwitz prisoners were likely, then, to die either way. But before they did, their job earned profits for the Nazi state and its friends. In late 1940 Nazi-connected businesses began taking advantage of all the cheap labor the party was making available to them.

Himmler and other Nazi officials, determined to exploit their captive populations for industrial labor to support the war effort, encouraged chemical corporation I.G. Farben and other industrialists to build plants near the death camps.

Auschwitz III, also known as Buna or Monowice, opened in October 1942. It housed primarily prisoners who worked at I.G. Farben's synthetic rubber works plant, located near the Polish town of Monowice. The conglomerate constructed the factory in the town for the express purpose of using laborers from the camp and making a profit. It invested heavily in the venture and agreed to pay a daily sum of three or four reichsmarks per worker per day, depending on how educated or skilled the worker was. These amounts were roughly equivalent to 75 percent of the wage a typical German worker received. But the prisoners were never actually paid for their slave labor; instead, Farben sent this money directly to Hitler's treasury.

Thirty-nine other sub-camps were put into use near the Auschwitz complex between 1942 and 1944. These served the various businesses, including Farben. The smaller facilities included coal mines, stone quarries, and armament factories that supplied the German military.

Other work consisted of burying the bodies of the dead. In the camp's early months, Commandant Höss struggled over what to do with thousands of rotting corpses. Initially, they were buried

Women prisoners line up for a hard labor assignment at Auschwitz.

in a field, but the holes were not deep enough and the summer heat made the smell of rotting flesh unbearable. Auschwitz survivor Otto Pressburger remembers: "We had to dig the bodies out and burn them. A big fire was made here with wood and petrol and we were throwing them right into it. There were always two of us throwing the bodies in, one holding the legs and one on the arms. The smell and the stench were terrible. The bodies were not only bloody but rotten as well. We were given some rags to put over our faces."[46]

Medical Experimentation

Not all of those saved from immediate extermination at Auschwitz were put to work. SS guards, at Mengele's direction, watched carefully as new prisoners stepped from the boxcars. Identical twins and people with genetic abnormalities such as dwarfism were often taken aside and told to see camp doctors for better treatment. Parents of children in these categories readily agreed to what they believed would be special care. Adults in these categories sometimes volunteered themselves, assuming they too would be spared the miserable conditions of the slave laborers.

These new patients kept their civilian clothes and stayed in Barracks 14 of Camp F, which was far cleaner and more accommodating than those in the other parts of the camp. Food here tasted good and there was plenty of it. Before long, the medical exams began. Patients had their blood taken, their ears checked, and their blood pressure gauged. The camp artist—known only as Dina—sketched many of them for the camp's records. Mengele insisted on it.

As a captain in the *Waffen-SS*, Mengele earned a stellar reputation among his superiors in the Third Reich, and on May 30, 1943, he arrived at Auschwitz as the camp's chief doctor.

Physicians are trained to aid humankind: study patients, determine ailments, and suggest treatments. But in the topsy-turvy world of Auschwitz, Mengele and the doctors on his staff made "patients" ill intentionally to observe how their already fragile bodies responded to pain, disease, and physical torment.

Because of his unique set of interests, Mengele's experiments were often different than those performed elsewhere. At places like Buchenwald concentration camp, Nazi doctors injected prisoners with biological diseases such as typhus or smallpox or yellow fever to take note of how their bodies responded. But Mengele's obsession with twins led to his attempts to change their eye color with chemicals and surgically change fraternal twins into Siamese twins. In one experiment, Mengele performed an autopsy on a one-year-old triplet while the child was still alive.

Historian Gretchen Engle Schafft writes about the difference between Mengele's placid and attractive exterior and his merciless cruelty: "He moved in an elegant fashion, always carefully dressed in uniform. . . . A kindergarten was set up, and the children received special rations. They routinely called him 'Uncle' or even 'Papa.' This behavior stood in stark contrast to his absolutely emotionless approach to experiments."[47]

Nazi ideology was founded upon the principle that the Nordic race was superior to all others. Mengele's ghoulish experiments existed to support his belief in "race science," including the idea that the Jewish race was genetically inferior to other people. Mengele chose twins for many sadistic, unethical experiments. He wanted to show that physically changing one twin by brutal medical procedures could not change that person's genetic makeup compared with the other twin.

Physician Miklos Nyiszli, a prisoner forced to work for Mengele to stay alive, autopsied Mengele's victims on a regular basis. Hoping that his work for the Nazi doctor would result in the lives of his wife and daughter also being spared, Nyiszli soon faced Mengele's horrific work. While performing autopsies on four pairs of twins from the Gypsy Camp, each of whom was less than ten years old, Nyiszli discovered all of them had a tiny pinprick hole in the left ventricles of their hearts. "The victim had received an injection of chloroform in the heart, so that the blood of the ventricle . . . would deposit on the valves and cause instantaneous death by heart failure."[48] Victims already sick or made sick by the doctors

Picture Perfect: An Auschwitz Album

The United States Holocaust Museum received a carefully wrapped package in January 2007: an old but well-maintained photo album with "Auschwitz 21.6.1944" inscribed on its first page. Although the identity of its original owner was unclear, the photographs inside presented a stark portrait of the death center. Here, in a series of candid black and white pictures, were Nazis at leisure, singing, eating blueberries. These, the private mementos of Karl Höcker, loyal adjutant to Auschwitz commandant Rudolf Höss, opened a window to the camp never seen before. Many of the photographs were taken at Solahütte, an SS retreat on the grounds of Auschwitz itself. The "Angel of Death," Josef Mengele, appears, as does Höss, along with SS women who worked in camp communications. Many of them smile or laugh, as if out on a picnic. Holocaust Museum researcher Rebecca Erbelding remains unsettled by the grainy pictures. Not by what they say about these people, responsible for so much death, pain, and misery, but what they might suggest about all of us: "They don't look like monsters. They look like me. They look like my next door neighbor. Is he capable of that? Am I?"

Quoted in United States Holocaust Museum, "Auschwitz Through the Lens of the SS: Photos of Nazi Leadership at the Camp." www.ushmm.org/museum/exhibit/online/ssalbum/?content=1.

in the camp "infirmary" were rarely treated except by this injection to the heart.

During his tenure at Auschwitz, Mengele sickened, disfigured, or killed over three thousand pairs of twins. His reputation at Auschwitz earned him the ominous nickname "Angel of Death."

Murder

Prisoners died in many ways at Auschwitz: shooting, starving, disease. But these methods involved uncertainty: Death did not always fit a timetable, and the system was therefore not effi-cient. The Nazis' preferred method of killing—the gas chamber—left nothing to chance and sped up the killing process.

Although the first Zyklon B tests were done at Auschwitz I, Birkenau quickly became the primary killing center. In late February 1942, Höss ordered his architect and head of the SS buildings office to move a planned body disposal center, or crematorium, from Auschwitz I to Birkenau. At the same time, the three men decided to use an old farmer's cottage on the grounds as a makeshift gas chamber. Known as "the Little Red House," or "Bunker 1," the cottage earned its name after workers bricked up all of its windows and doors. The house's inner walls, kitchen, and other areas were removed and replaced with two new sealed spaces. New entryways were also created, as was a small hatch near the top of the brickwork for the Zyklon B pellets. The deadly poison was manufactured in Frankfurt, Germany, by German Pesticide Systems (DEGESH), a subsidiary of I.G. Farben.

"The Little Red House" became Auschwitz-Birkenau's first fully functioning gas chamber. Only weeks later, a second site, "the Little White House" or Bunker 2, went into operation. Here, rooms were smaller and narrower, but the bunker had four of them, and the ventilation was better. Twelve hundred people at one time could be gassed here.

The victims were first shown into a room and were told to remove their clothes and hang them on hooks. As inmates undressed, SS often encouraged them to remember their prison numbers and to hurry so they would not be too late to enjoy the hot coffee that awaited them after their warm shower. But once ushered into the showers, many prisoners sensed that something was wrong.

A gas chamber at Auschwitz. Victims were led into the chamber believing they were going to receive a shower.

The Ovitz family is pictured in 1949. These siblings were spared death because Nazi doctor Josef Mengele performed medical experiments on identical twins and people with genetic abnormalities such as dwarfism.

Prisoner Sam Itzkowitz recalls the gas chambers at Auschwitz, in part because he helped build them. He describes a hall with two chimneys. First, the women were led in; then the men entered:

> Sometimes they had 20 or 30 extra people that they couldn't get in, so they always held back the children . . . [then] they made the kids crawl on top of the heads, all the way in there, just kept on pushing them in, to fill them all in. When the door was slammed behind them, was a thick door, was about six inches thick. I built it myself and I know what it's like: three bolts, three iron bolts were across. The bars were laid over and then screwed tight.[49]

Standing outside the building, Karl Lill got to see what happened next. In sworn testimony, the former prisoner and assistant to one of the camp physicians said he watched as the doctor and his helpers "climbed onto the flat roof of the bunker. . . . He put on a gas mask. So did his helpers. They opened the can of Zyklon B and threw the contents into these hatches. And every time, a few seconds later, a cry, muffled by the concrete ceiling, a scream in unison of a hundred or more voices. Every time, a few minutes later, a brown, a brownish yellow fume came out of the smokestack.[50]

In ten to twenty minutes, it was all over.

Raphael Lemkin: The Father of "Genocide"

Raphael Lemkin did not invent genocide. The murder of innocents based on their ethnicity or difference is almost as old as mankind itself. But Lemkin did coin the term in 1943 by melding the Greek word *genos*, meaning "tribe, race or family" with the Latin *–cide*, meaning "killing." Yet Lemkin, a tireless advocate for human rights, accomplished much more than that in his fifty-nine years. Born into a Polish-Jewish family in what is now Lithuania, Lemkin took an early interest in the fates of cultures, especially the undeclared Armenian genocide by the Turks in the years before World War I. He later wrote how, from a young age, he "was appalled by the frequency of evil . . . and by the impunity coldly relied upon by the guilty." After earning his law degree, Lemkin worked as the public prosecutor in Warsaw, Poland, from 1929 to 1934. There he helped rewrite and redefine the Polish penal code and lectured before the League of Nations on criminal law. In 1939 he saw action in the Polish army and defended the country against the Nazi onslaught. Still, forty-nine members of his family died in the Holocaust. His best known book, *Axis Rule in Occupied Europe*, argues for international laws against genocide. He spent the rest of his life trying to get such laws passed, with mixed success.

Quoted in Samantha Power, *"A Problem from Hell": America and the Age of Genocide.* New York: Harper Perennial, 2002, p. 20.

During the height of the deportations in 1943 and 1944, from forty-seven hundred up to as many as eight thousand Jews died this way daily at Auschwitz and Auschwitz-Birkenau, but Yehuda Bacon was not one of them. Bacon entered Auschwitz as a teenager with his mother, father, and cousins. On cold winter days he and a group of other teens and children shoveled ash from the crematoria onto the snow so prisoners and guards could walk without slipping. When they were finished, he says, if the Kapo was in a good mood, he and the others were allowed to sit in the warmth of the vacant gas chambers. He later drew sketches of the chambers from memory: "I took a close look at it all," he recalls. "For instance, the showers interested me because I saw there weren't any real holes [for the water]."[51]

Disposal

Like a well-oiled assembly line, Auschwitz had become a factory with a single product: death. By now, the sprawling, multi-camp operation had murdered over 1 million people. From the outset, as bodies piled upon bodies—mothers, fathers, and children—disposal became an issue. Burial had not worked—too messy—and Höss was desperate for relief from the staggering number of corpses. In the fall of 1941, the Zyklon B experiments in Block 11 were moved to the camp crematorium situated near Höss's office and the other administration buildings. Now the bodies, rather than be carted through the camp, could be disposed of at the same location.

Then, in March 1943 the first crematorium opened in Auschwitz I, replacing "the Little Red House." In this new location, with the gas chamber located in the basement and three large ovens on the ground floor each capable of burning five bodies each, Höss seemed confident that Auschwitz could begin dealing with the overwhelming numbers of dead. His confidence rose further that summer when four more crematoria/gas chambers went into operation at Auschwitz-Birkenau to accommodate this factory of death.

Crematoria 2 and 3 were located less than 109 yards (100m) from a planned Birkenau "ramp," much like the one functioning in Auschwitz I. Two others, crematoria 4 and 5, placed near "the Little Red House" and "the Little White House," contained the gas chambers and crematoria on the same floor. Thus, transporting the cadavers became far easier. Here, one large oven with eight furnace doors provided enormous burning power. All told, by the summer of 1943 the four new crematoria could murder and dispose of 4,400 people daily, or 120,000 per month. (The first

crematorium, at Auschwitz I, was shut down in 1943 when the capacity at Birkenau was so greatly enlarged.)

By this time, writes Laurence Rees, "Auschwitz was of growing importance in the Nazi state . . . it was obvious to men like Himmler that the only installation in the Nazi empire capable of satisfactorily uniting the twin goals of work and murder was Auschwitz."[52] But by 1944 transports from some areas in Europe had slowed as remaining Jewish populations were systematically destroyed. The Nazis now looked to other countries such as Hungary for fresh victims, and zealous officers such as Adolf Eichmann used any and all methods to send as many people to the camps as possible. The war was going badly for Hitler; the growing conviction that Germany's defeat was imminent only made Eichmann and his fellow officials more determined to speed up the killing process.

The Nazis were aided in achieving their goals by their practice of forcing prisoners themselves to do the horrific tasks involved in murder and body disposal, which also allowed camp administrators to distance themselves from the barbarity of their actions. Camp inmates were organized in squads called *Sonderkommandos*, or "special units." Their work came after the gassing itself, which took no more than fifteen to twenty minutes. Once completed, electric ventilators were turned on to rid the chamber of the poisonous gas and, said one member of the unit, "With trembling hands our [Sonderkommando] brethren now remove bolts and raise four bolts. Two doors opened now—of the two large tombs. A wave of cruel death struck, inflicting profound agony. . . . They have been silenced forever. Their gazes remained frozen, their bodies prostrate, motionless."[53] Typically the bodies were massed together, one piled upon the other. In the chaos, victims had stepped on one another, clawed at each other and the chamber walls to try to climb away from the gas that poured in through the lower reaches of the whitewashed room. The physically weaker victims—women, children, and the aged—were at the bottom of the pile. At the moment of death, human beings lose control of all body functions and defecate and urinate on themselves. A Sonderkommando squad stood ready in rubber boots and holding hoses, which they turned on to wash the bodies now caked with blood and excrement. Sometimes they sprayed perfume they had found among the clothing of murdered women; the next group of victims must remain unaware of their looming fate.

The Sonderkommandos then carted the bodies from the chamber. First, they took them to the "tooth-pulling" squad, located directly in front of the ovens. Here, eight skilled inmates—each equipped with pliers and a lever—extracted gold fillings from the victims'

Prisoners place a human corpse into a furnace at the concentration camp in Auschwitz.

teeth and tossed them in a bucket full of acid. This separated the fillings from any gum or bone. Nyiszli estimated that 18 to 20 pounds (8 to 9kg) of gold were taken each day from the dead to enrich Nazi coffers.

The victims' bodies were loaded into the ovens, which at peak periods ran twenty-four hours a day. Cremation took about twenty minutes. The smell of burning flesh from the crematoria permeated the camp and dark smoke shot into the sky. Sonderkommandos carted the ashes to trucks, which were driven to the nearby Vistula River or swampy fields. Here, the ashes were dumped.

By 1944 the Nazis had perfected their assembly line of death, from deportation to disposal. Their commitment to destroying the Jews of Europe and hiding evidence of that destruction is unrivaled in the history of humankind. Those not immediately led to their deaths at Auschwitz struggled against succumbing to it every day. Many who survived speak of their will to live, the kindness of a stranger, or the sheer luck that saved them, even when all hope seemed lost.

Chapter Four

Surviving Auschwitz

For the living dead of Auschwitz—the roughly 10 percent of arrivals not sent directly to the gas chambers—survival was an ambiguous concept. Meager rations coupled with slave labor tested their physical limits and caused untold suffering. The knowledge that they could be sent to the gas chambers at any moment or shot on a guard's whim, and perhaps that loved ones had already met such a fate, caused untold emotional suffering. Witnessing the daily humiliation and degradation their fellows were subjected to, as well as atrocities committed with impunity, broke the spirit.

For the inmates, Auschwitz was largely a world unto itself. Whispers that the Germans were losing the war and that Auschwitz would soon be liberated seemed but a dream. For the thousands who died of starvation or disease while awaiting liberation, it was. Bodies littered the camp; trash was everywhere. Survivors speak of becoming numb to the sight of death, which surrounded them at all times. Even the smell of burning flesh from the crematoria became only one more surreal aspect of the camp in which they moved about like ghosts.

At All Costs

As prisoners' bodies withered, so too did the normal sense of right and wrong. Stealing among the population was common, as was betrayal of fellow prisoners. Collaboration with the SS could mean the difference between longer life and immediate destruction.

While many inmates considered prisoners in the Sonderkommando to be traitors for their part in burning bodies and working in the Auschwitz "infirmary," the squad members themselves had struck a bargain they hoped would delay their own extermination. In return for their participation, they ate better

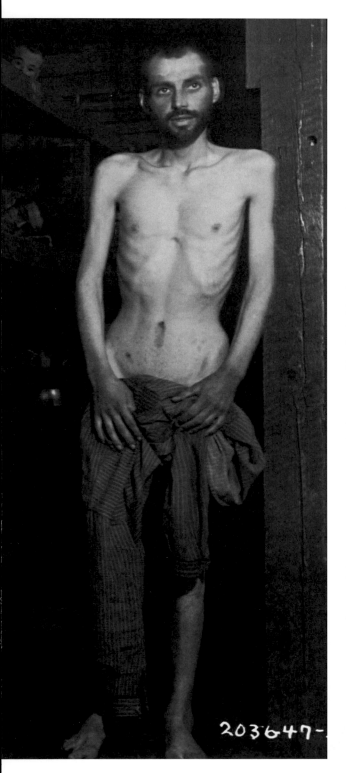

food, were housed in livable barracks, and wore civilian clothes. They also had access to Nazi commanders that many others did not have.

When Miklos Nyiszli, a skilled physician, realized that his wife and daughter would soon be gassed, he bribed an SS officer to have his family transferred to a women's work unit. Still he, like other Sonderkommando members, knew that after but a few months in the service of his jailers, he would also be gassed and burned.

In desperate times humans look for ways to survive, even temporarily. Their methods and morals may differ, but in the harshness of Auschwitz, prisoners were often forced to make choices they never imagined they would have to.

Other prisoners resisted any threat to their sense of humanity or morality. Auschwitz survivor Primo Levi wrote extensively about his Holocaust experience. In one noted passage in his best known work, *If This Is a Man* (also titled *Survival in Auschwitz*), Levi, an Italian chemist sent to Auschwitz in February 1944, remembers arguing with a fellow inmate about hygiene. What was the purpose of washing yourself, Levi had asked, when you were about to die? The other prisoner, Steinlauf, told him that because the Nazis' goal was to dehumanize them, it was their job to resist as much as possible and not give in, either

Inmates were forced to sleep on bunk beds made of boards, which slept five or six people each.

to the Nazis or to the temptations to degrade themselves: "We must not become beasts . . . even in this place one can survive, and therefore one must want to survive, to tell the story, to bear witness. . . . We are slaves, deprived of every right, exposed to every insult, condemned to certain death, but we still possess one power—the power to refuse our consent."[54]

Shelter, Food, and Disease

By 1943 Nazi Germany's ambition had clearly outstripped its ability to fight a war on numerous fronts. Inmates of the camp longed to hear any word that the Third Reich could be defeated. But Auschwitz remained a world within the world—an inferno of pain and misery and sickness without light, joy, or, seemingly, a road out.

Often alone, separated from their families, prisoners at Auschwitz looked for a way—any way—to survive just one more day. Before being placed in Auschwitz I or Auschwitz II, prisoners spent time in BIIa, the quarantine camp. Here, they learned the discipline and the rules of the inferno they had entered.

In or out of quarantine, the long, wooden barracks in which inmates lived did not make survival easy. Bunk beds made from boards slept five or six people each. A narrow brick stove ran the length of the barracks between the bunks. Survivor Stella Marcus recalls that "the barracks was a huge block, and the walls were lined with three shelves, with one cubby for every six people to sleep in. If one person turned, everyone had to turn. There were no blankets. The latrine was a big trough with wooden planks with holes."[55]

The toilets were little more than large outhouses, and prisoners had to clean them out with shovels when filled. There was no toilet paper. Yet prisoners coveted the work because SS never entered the latrines and inmates could, therefore, discuss escape plans or trade cigarettes or food. Latrine workers also stank so badly from their jobs that SS left them alone.

At or before dawn each day a loud bell woke camp workers, and SS men drove their captives out of the barracks for roll call. Those who had died during the night lay in their beds or on the ground, soon to be carted to the crematoria. Before roll call, prisoners had to exercise regardless of how sick or feeble they were or how cold or hot it was outside.

The roll call itself could last hours, and prisoners sometimes died during it. Those who survived long enough for their breakfast ration received 10 ounces (0.3kg) of bread with a bit of salami or margarine and weak coffee. Survivor Heniek Sztarkman says that "food was always a problem. Always. You were constantly hungry. Later on, as conditions became worse towards the end, there were sometimes periods of three days when there was no food to be had at all."[56]

After a twelve-hour day at work in the camps or one of the sub-camps, prisoners returned to a dinner of watery

Anne Frank at Auschwitz

Perhaps the most famous chronicle of life during wartime is the diary kept by Anne Frank, a young Jewish girl living in Amsterdam during World War II. After having their hiding place discovered by the Nazis, the Frank family was arrested. And on September 3, 1944, Anne, her mother, Edith, father, Otto, and sister Margot were sent by train to Auschwitz-Birkenau. Two days later the Franks arrived along with 1,019 others. As was typical, women and men were immediately separated from one another and tattooed. Camp doctors then decided who would live and who would die. Anne's family, along with eight others from the secret annex who had arrived with them, were spared the gas chambers and put to work. Eight weeks later, as the Soviets advanced, nervous Nazi leaders stuffed healthy prisoners onto a freight train and sent them to Bergen-Belsen in Germany. Anne and Margot, heads shaved and hungry, were among those chosen. Their mother remained, dying in January 1945. The three-day train journey to the new camp further weakened the young women. Although briefly reunited with Auguste van Pels, one of their annex mates, the winter of 1944 was especially harsh for them: Food was scarce, and conditions were filthy and encouraged disease. Before long the sisters contracted typhus and died. Only weeks later, the Allies liberated Bergen-Belsen.

Anne Frank is pictured, along with a page from her diary. Frank, along with her father, mother, and sister arrived in Auschwitz in early September 1944, but only her father survived that winter.

soup. The poor diets and the lack of sanitary conditions at Auschwitz meant disease was endemic. Ironically, the SS often wrote reminders on barracks rafters, including *Sauberheit = Gesundheit*, or "cleanliness equals good health."

Despite the pleasant prompt, prisoners constantly scratched their heads, their clothes—the result of lice. "We were infested with lice," says survivor Alice Lok Cahana, "and it felt so horrible—horrible. Nothing can be so humiliating as when you feel your whole body is infested. Your head, your clothes—everywhere you look on your body there's an animal crawling. And you cannot wash it off. There's no water."[57] Rats and bedbugs also had to be contended with.

Such unsanitary conditions bred sickness. Common—and often deadly—ailments included typhus and dysentery. Most prisoners suffered from diarrhea. Although the numbers of people who died from disease alone at Auschwitz are uncertain, nearly 50 percent of deaths at Auschwitz were caused by something other than gassing, often during the night.

In the morning, inmates would often awake to find their bunkmate dead or near dead. "Death, death, death," is how a former Russian POW described it. "Death at night, death in the morning, death in the afternoon. Death. We lived with death. How could a human feel?"[58]

"Winter Relief Mission"

An ongoing task in the operations at Auschwitz took place in a section of Auschwitz-Birkenau known as "Canada," a large warehouse where inmate workers sorted through victims' pants, jackets, briefcases, and even underwear looking for money, diamonds, and anything else of significance. When one of the mostly female workers found something of worth, she slipped it into a wooden box; it now belonged to the Reich. Heaps of possessions—coats, socks, hats—were then carted to trucks marked "Winter Relief Mission," to be distributed to German soldiers on the eastern front.

Many workers in "Canada" considered themselves lucky, as they were better fed than those in other parts of the camp. They also got to keep their hair. But thievery became the norm, as both workers and the SS smuggled items out of the building.

As former Slovak inmate Rudolf Vrba sees it, "No one was murdered without being robbed. As someone who saw Auschwitz from the inside, I can assure you that it was about robbery. Murder was a byproduct, a means to an end."[59]

SS member Oskar Groening, who worked in the Economic Agency, became known as "King of the Dollars." His job included counting and collating stolen money for the Third Reich, but Groening also lined his own pockets with wads of foreign currency. His dishonesty and thievery was not unique.

Stolen valuables and cash became such an issue in the camp that by October 1943, Himmler drew a distinction between what he considered justifiable murder and the crime of stealing. Riches diverted and crimes committed to support the Nazi state were acceptable, but

During the "Winter Relief Mission" at Auschwitz, inmates were forced to give up their coats, socks, and hats for German soldiers.

individual theft for personal gain was unacceptable, dishonorable, and harshly punished. According to Rees, "For them [the Nazis] to be able to live with themselves . . . he had to paint a picture of the SS members as killers of women and children, yes, but murderers who had still retained their honor."[60]

Nazis and Jews: The Razor's Edge

Nazi honor and morality also came into question when personal relationships sometimes developed between SS and inmates. For most members of the Third Reich, including the charming and handsome Mengele, the thought of a sexual relationship between a "racially superior" Nazi and a "lowly" Jew was an abomination.

Yet the reality at Auschwitz was more complex, as Groening explained: "If one is in a routine where one is looking after twenty young girls and one is a favorite and making coffee and God knows what, then these things, these propagandistic things, they aren't important anymore."[61]

Women working in Canada were the most frequent targets. There, women ate better and suffered from less disease than in the other parts of Auschwitz. They also looked more like the typical women an SS member might see on the outside since their heads were not shaved and they wore their own clothes. Reports of rape, while not common, were not unheard of.

Likewise, in Birkenau, women placed in the "family camp" were susceptible to sexual abuse by their guards. The "family camp," created in September 1943, contained eighteen thousand people deported from the Theresienstadt ghetto in Czechoslovakia. The Nazis intended to use these prisoners, separated from other inmates by barbed wire fences, as propaganda. "Family camp" captives were told to write letters home telling family and friends that, despite the rumors, they were being treated well by the Nazis. But Ruth Elias remembers the abuse of women here by drunken SS who entered her barracks and chose women to take with them: "The girls came back crying," Elias says, "they had been raped. They were in a terrible state."[62]

Józef Paczyński, an inmate since 1940, almost considered Auschwitz a kind of home and made a life for himself as barber for the SS staff. Unlike most, Paczyński came in close contact

A woman and her children at the Birkenau family camp. Women in this camp were more likely to be abused by Nazi guards because they looked less like the typical concentration camp prisoners.

with camp commandant Höss and at least once visited his house to give him a trim:

> Höss came in and sat down. I stood at attention. He had a cigar in his mouth and was reading a paper. I did the same haircut I had seen done on him before. Höss didn't say a word to me, and I didn't say a word. I was afraid, and he despised inmates. I had a razor in my hand. I could have cut his throat. . . . But I'm a thinking being, and you know what would have happened? My whole family would have been destroyed. . . . In his place someone else would have come.[63]

In rare cases, Nazis and their family members showed signs of compassion for the suffering hordes. SS men lived at Auschwitz; officers also lived there, but typically with their families. Paczyński's bunkmate, Stasiu Dubiel, worked at Höss's home as a gardener. Paczyński had long admired the commandant's vegetable garden, which sat not far from one of the crematoria. After his friend Stasiu showed him the best way to reach it and get some fresh greens, Paczyński stole into the garden and stuffed some vegetables into his pockets. But on the way out, he ran into Höss's wife and was certain he would be killed for the transgression.

Yet later, Stasiu told Paczyński that he had taken the blame for the theft. Stasiu and Frau Höss knew one another and he was useful to her. She saw nothing wrong with him taking some of her vegetables, and the matter was forgotten. For many inmates, this kind of experience was the key to survival. If the Nazis considered you of use to them, you lived, at least for a while.

Escape and Resistance

With their tight security and barbed wire fencing, Auschwitz I and Auschwitz II (Birkenau) made escape seem foolhardy but not impossible. In the camp's first year of operation, only one escape was attempted. In 1941 seventeen other escape plans were hatched but did not succeed. From then on, attempts skyrocketed, reaching a high in 1944 with 312, according to camp records. Earlier, since most of the prisoners were Poles, there was a chance that fugitives could actually get away. Civilians in the Polish countryside surrounding Auschwitz were likely to be sympathetic to the inmates' plight. If only they could breach the perimeter fence—called Grosse Postenkette—they might blend in with locals. Prevention came by way of example; those who tried to escape and were caught were tortured. If not caught, prisoners' families or block mates would bear the brunt of the punishment.

One high-profile escape occurred only weeks before a visit from Himmler in 1942. Planned by Polish political prisoner Kazimierz Piechowski, the idea called for obtaining a set of SS uniforms. But neither Piechowski nor his coconspirators could figure out how to get them. Then, a stroke of luck.

This sign, in front of Auschwitz's barbed wire fence, warns of "high voltage." Escape from the camp was rare because of the tight security that surrounded the site.

For the Record

For over sixty years the records of 17 million people interned by the Nazis were kept locked away in storerooms in the German town of Bad Arolsen. German officials claimed they were protecting the privacy of the victims. But in 2007 the sixteen miles of shelves were opened to the public for the first time. Here, visitors can peruse arrest warrants and personal documents that paint a detailed picture of life under Nazi rule. Although the Nazis methodically destroyed the files of those sent to the gas chambers, the Bad Arolsen archive does contain "Deathbooks," which note the fates of people who died of disease and starvation. For aging survivors of the Holocaust, the archive opens a window into the past and once again brings them face to face with the evil humans can do. Miki Schwartz was fourteen when he watched his parents being led to the gas chambers. Confronted with his young self on paper, Schwartz says, "It makes me think back, and I'm living like there is this 14-year-old youngster and they wanted to kill him. I don't know why, I did not ever do anything, any harm to anybody. I think I should have a middle name, my middle name to be Mr. Lucky."

Quoted in CBS News, "Revisiting the Horrors of the Holocaust," *60 Minutes*, June 24, 2007. www.cbsnews.com/stories/2006/12/14/60minutes/main2267927.shtml.

Piechowski's Kapo told him to retrieve boxes from one of the rooms in the warehouse in which he worked. While looking for them, he came across a room that read "uniforms."

Days later, Piechowski found the door unlocked. He pushed the door open but found an SS man working inside. He received a beating from the guard and was ordered to report to the main office. Knowing that if he did as he was told he would be killed, Piechowski did nothing and hoped the Nazi guard would forget about the incident. He did.

Then, on Saturday, June 20, 1942, a day off for SS men in the warehouse, Piechowski and his small crew took a chance. First, they donned their stolen SS uniforms and filched four machine guns and eight hand grenades from a storage area. They hopped into a car another member of the group had acquired and drove toward the main gate. Along the way, they played the part of loyal soldiers, raising their arms and shouting "Heil Hitler" as SS men rolled by. They had no documents to support their roles as Nazis; they hoped they would not need them.

They drove slowly toward the gate, but it did not open: 90 yards (80m), 50 yards (46m), 10 yards (9m)—the gate remained down. Piechowski says he considered killing himself. Instead, not wanting to let the others down, "I yelled at the SS: 'How long are we going to be waiting here!' I cursed them. And then the SS man at the watchtower said something and he opened the gate and we went through. That was freedom."[64]

In his book Night, *Nobel Prize–winning writer Elie Wiesel writes about how his confinement at Auschwitz caused him to lose his faith.*

Faith in Auschwitz

According to the testimony of countless survivors, traumatized inmates often became numb to the horrors of the death camp and abandoned deeply held principles. Many lost their faith in God. The daily desire to retain one's humanity and the desire to live often passed away before the physical death of the prisoner occurred. Others, though, looked inward to try to find the strength to go on. David Weiss Halivni grew up in Romania and by sixteen was a noted student of Judaism. He planned on becoming a rabbi, but the Nazis had other plans: In 1944 they arrested Halivni, his grandfather, mother, sister, and aunt and sent them to Auschwitz.

Fellow camp members were impressed with the boy's knowledge of the Talmud and Torah, Judaism's most sacred texts, yet Auschwitz challenged his faith: "Since there were so many cruelties," he thought, "God cannot exist. He would not have permitted it. But without God it is even more cruel."

Soon after arriving at Auschwitz, Halivni was transferred to the Gross-Rosen camp in Germany, where he worked cutting stones for roads with a team of men. In the few off hours allotted them, some of the men recited Hebrew texts from memory, since books were forbidden. One day, Halivni noticed a guard eating a sandwich wrapped in a *bletl*, part of a religious text. "Seeing the bletl," he says, "I fell at his feet with tears in my eyes and begged, 'Please give it to me.' He put his hand on his revolver—but after a few moments, he gave the bletl to me." Halivni considered this a sign from God, a reward for his faith. Halivni became the only member of his family to survive Auschwitz. Millions of others, regardless of their faith, did not.

Quoted in Toby Axelrod, *In the Camps: Teens Who Survived the Nazi Concentration Camps.* New York: Rosen, 1999, p. 23.

Outside the dreaded gates of Auschwitz, the four drove through the Polish countryside to a place where friends helped them get rid of their Nazi uniforms and the stolen car. The men soon blended in with the local population until the war was over.

Such daring escapes were rare but not unheard of. Less common, though, were outright rebellions. Camp SS kept tight control over their charges, and with the hated Sonderkommandos working for them, uprisings within Auschwitz were extraordinarily difficult to pull off.

As in many oppressive situations, though, an underground resistance to the camp system developed at Auschwitz. Highly secretive, it aimed to undermine Nazi power and ultimately free as many inmates as possible. Ironically, the more noted attempts at rebellion were led by inmates in the Sonderkommandos themselves. In June 1944 a group of them planned a revolt, even enlisting the help of prisoner Yaacov Kamiński, a resistance leader. But the uneasy alliance between kommando and Kamiński's resisters did not hold. After the plan was revealed and Kamiński executed, the Nazi collaborators and the underground resistance worked separately. The core of Kamiński's group continued what he started. They stockpiled tools, food, weapons—anything they could find in hope that they would one day be able to use them.

The Sonderkommando inmates continued plotting too. The Nazis typically murdered their prison helpers after only a few months of work as a way of ensuring the relative secrecy of the gas chambers. But as hope for Nazi victory in the war diminished and the likelihood that advancing Russian armies would liberate the Polish camps increased, Sonderkommandos realized that, like their fellow prisoners, death could come at any time. This compelled the Twelfth Sonderkommando to act. For months, female prisoners smuggled them gunpowder, which the men used to make grenades out of sardine cans. They also gathered knives and axes.

The initial plan called for a revolt to coincide with the approach of the Soviet army, but they could not wait that long. On October 7, 1944, the Polish and Hungarian Sonderkommandos in Crematorium 4 attacked SS men with axes and rocks. Then they set the building on fire. The Sonderkommandos in Crematorium 2 saw the flames and determined the uprising had begun. Russian prisoners grabbed one hated Kapo and wrestled him into an oven and burned him alive.

But before other prisoners could join the rebellion, Nazi guards fought back and brutally suppressed what became known as the largest revolt in the camp's history. In the end, 250 Sonderkommando inmates were captured and told to lie face down outside the crematoria, where they each received one bullet to the brain. The women who helped them obtain the gunpowder were hanged.

Red Flowers

For certain prisoners, surviving Auschwitz almost became a game of willful self-delusion. Fifteen-year-old Alice Lok Cahana never tried to escape. Instead, she was intent on remaining close to her sister, Edith, and helping her survive.

One summer during their imprisonment, Edith came down with typhoid fever. The camp hospital was typically off limits to other prisoners, but Alice bribed a Kapo with bread and helped him carry dead bodies. In return, she got to see her beloved sister, whom she visited almost every day.

Alice also began making up stories about the war ending and the prisoners being freed. Despite her attempts at fantasy, Alice realized that sick prisoners did not last long at Auschwitz, as they were usually sent to the gas chambers. She devised a plan and told Edith, "If you can just bear it, I will take you out as a dead person and then we'll go back to our barrack."[65]

Edith played dead, and Alice carried her from the hospital, as she had done with so many other bodies. Back at their barracks, it became difficult to hide Edith among the healthy women. In October 1944, the two were "selected." Alice remembers being taken to "a nice building with flowers in the windows,"[66] where the inmates were told to take off their clothes and wait for instructions; they would receive warm clothes after their shower. But after a few moments, an SS woman suddenly opened the doors and screamed for the naked women to get out. Alice protested that she had not received the promised warm clothes. Her fellow prisoners were in disbelief: Didn't she know where she was and that she had, by luck, escaped death that day?

Although she lived in sight of the gas chambers, Alice says that she had other things on her mind:

I was so focused on Edith that all the energy I could muster was on how to keep her alive. So that kind of fear didn't occur to me—maybe it was so horrendous you couldn't comprehend. . . . In our house you could never utter an ugly word. So how can you imagine something so foul that they kill people this way? And we were always taught that the Germans were a civilized people.[67]

All these years later, Alice's most vivid memory is of the red geraniums growing in the window boxes outside the crematorium. "See flowers in a window—reminding you of home," she says. "Reminding you that mother went out when the Germans came into Hungary, and instead of being scared . . . she went to the market and bought violets. And it made me so calm. If mother buys flowers it can't be so bad. They will not hurt us."[68]

Such sentiments illustrate the surreal quality of life in Auschwitz. Surrounded on all sides by death and inhumanity, prisoners survived in any way they could. For Alice Lok Cahana, self-deception provided her a sense that all would be well; for others, plotting insurrection provided a chance, however small, at escape and revenge. What few prisoners knew by the fall of 1944 was that deliverance was at hand.

Chapter Five

Liberation and Aftermath

After D-day, the successful Allied landing in Normandy on June 6, 1944, it was becoming clear that German forces were in retreat and Germany's defeat was inevitable. Hitler still issued stirring promises of victory, but he appeared less and less frequently in public, and his chain of command became increasingly disorganized.

At Auschwitz, the Sonderkommando uprising led not only to the deaths of those involved but to the dismantling of the charred remains of Crematorium 4 on October 14, 1944. Less than two months later, on December 1, prisoners were ordered to pound dynamite holes into the walls of Birkenau's Crematorium 3.

The Third Reich's efforts to cover their deadly tracks became more desperate and chaotic. In January 1945, with the war all but lost, Himmler ordered the evacuation of all eastern camps. He wrote to his camp commanders: "The Führer holds you personally responsible for . . . making sure that not a single prisoner from the concentration camps falls alive into the hands of the enemy."[69]

Death March

On January 18, as the Soviet army approached, Auschwitz SS men gathered sixty-five thousand "fit" inmates in the wind and snow and told them to walk. Thus began the infamous death marches that would take the Nazi captors and their prey west into Germany. One group headed northwest through Mikolów, the other due west toward the Polish town of Wodzislaw. Prisoners who survived the journey often remember this portion of their Auschwitz experience as the worst ordeal of their captivity.

Prisoner Helena Citrónová watched her fellow captives fall in the first days of the march. "They didn't have any

Women march in a region of Czechoslovakia on the final day of a nearly five-hundred-mile death march that began on January 21, 1945, and ended on May 5. The women were forced to march in freezing weather without adequate food or shelter.

strength left and they died," she says. "Each person took care of himself. Total chaos. Whoever lived—lived. Whoever died—died."[70]

With the sounds of Soviet mortars exploding in the sky, the SS tried to maintain order by having the prisoners march in rows of five. But most could neither keep the order nor the pace, falling from lack of food and water. "They took them through the woods and they marched at night," says Benjamin Ferencz, a soldier who helped liberate the camps. "And if anybody faltered on the way they were immedi-

ately shot; if anybody paused to try to pick up a potato or to eat a root or something, they were shot."[71] Ferencz remembers being able to follow the trail of bodies for miles.

These ghastly three-week journeys continued at two railway stations, as prisoners were loaded into cattle cars. Morris Venezia, a Sonderkommando member, recalls a German prisoner who longed to sit. The German bartered cigarettes with Venezia for the privilege. But after Venezia had smoked the lot, he demanded the German stand again. The German refused; a trade was a trade.

Venezia "and a couple of friends we sat on him. And [after] about thirty minutes or one hour he was suffocated and we threw him out of the wagon. No problem. We were glad we killed a German."[72]

Author Laurence Rees sees Venezia's act of brutality as a "reminder of the debased moral landscape of the camp, and of how each prisoner was often forced to consider his or her own survival above all else."[73]

While the death marchers of Auschwitz boarded trains, and at least one took his anger out on a fellow prisoner, all over eastern Europe, in the vast network of Nazi concentration and death camps, similar scenes were being carried out. The mass exodus, an attempt by the retreating German army to keep hold of their valuable human resource, was in full swing.

Soviet Salvation

Meanwhile, the Soviet onslaught was fast approaching the infamous gates of Auschwitz. And one night, as the inmates slept, members of the SS blew up the Auschwitz-Birkenau crematoria.

The Bombing of Auschwitz

By the fall of 1944, 5 million Jews had been killed in concentration camps all across eastern Europe. According to government documents, the U.S. Air Force had the ability to bomb Auschwitz by the spring of 1944. Even earlier, they had targeted Nazi ally I.G. Farben's chemical and rubber plant, which employed slave labor from Auschwitz. But the Americans had indefinitely delayed military action for reasons unknown. Jewish leaders, including Zionist David Ben-Gurion, remained ambivalent, fearing that Allied bombing would doubtless kill not only Nazis but innocent Jews. Jacob Rosenheim, president of the Orthodox Agudas Israel World Organization seemed willing to take that risk. "Every day of delay," he wrote, "means a very heavy responsibility for the human lives at stake." But historian Robert N. Rosen argues that American president Franklin Delano Roosevelt knew little—if anything—about the plan to bomb Auschwitz, and typically left military decisions to his commanders in the field. Despite this version of events, many remain convinced that Roosevelt was well aware of such a bombing plan but, for reasons unknown, never gave the order to proceed. For them, Roosevelt's failure to save the Jews of Auschwitz casts a dark shadow on his presidency.

Quoted in Robert N. Rosen, *Saving the Jews: Franklin D. Roosevelt and the Holocaust.* New York: Thunder's Mouth, 2006, p. 384.

Then, on January 20 SS units were ordered to kill the weakest prisoners at Birkenau and Auschwitz sub-camps. But the Red Army was so near by now that the loyal SS abandoned their final orders in a last-ditch effort to save themselves.

"There was no sign of the Germans," says Bart Stern. "I wanted to go back to the barracks, but the Poles . . . the Ukraines, who were not taken on the death march, they wouldn't let me in. So I was hiding out in the heap of dead bodies . . . because I was afraid they'd [the Germans] come back or something."[74]

The Germans did not return. Soviet soldiers of the First Ukrainian Front, dressed in white camouflage, entered Auschwitz on January 27, 1945. A soldier at first believed Sam Itzkowitz to be a German, but once the soldier saw Itzkowitz's sorry physical state he realized what had happened. "He reached in his pocket and he pulled out a bar of chocolate. And he gave it to me," remembers Itzkowitz. "It was nourishing. I tried to bite into the doggone thing. I would swallow the whole thing if I could. I couldn't, so I sucked on it, and he just stood there and looked at me and looked at me."[75]

Eve Mozes Kor remembers running "up to them and they gave us hugs, cookies, and chocolates. Being so alone, a hug meant more than anybody could imagine, because that replaced the human worth we were starving for."[76]

The memories of American army nurse Pat Lynch provide a sense of the ragged people the liberators of Auschwitz saw before them. "They were so thin," remembers Lynch, who cared for other camp survivors likewise near death. "I couldn't pick any of them up. I tried to, but if I were to pick them up I'd tear the skin. So we had to be very, very careful moving them out."[77]

The Soviets found 6,000 survivors at Birkenau, 600 at Monowitz, and over 1,000 at Auschwitz I. In Auschwitz's massive warehouses, soldiers recovered hundreds of thousands of men's suits, more than 800,000 pieces of women's clothing, and over 14,000 pounds (6,350kg) of human hair.

Ironically, many soldiers in the Red Army, while moved by the devastation they saw before them, also put the experience in wider perspective. "I had seen towns being destroyed," says Ivan Martynushkin. "I had seen the destruction of villages. I had seen the suffering of our own people."[78] For now, at least, with the full measure of Nazi war crimes yet to be revealed and understood, Auschwitz seemed to represent only one more brutal chapter in the all-consuming war.

Bergen-Belsen and Himmler

Many Auschwitz survivors were still living that brutality. Their new camp, Bergen-Belsen, was an even greater horror. The camp, with roughly fifteen thousand inmates at the end of 1944, became overcrowded with sixty thousand by April 1945. The Nazis, unable or unwilling to accommodate their desperate

Soviet soldiers speak with some of the prisoners they liberated from Auschwitz. About seven thousand prisoners, including more than six hundred below the age of eighteen, were still alive when the camp was liberated.

prisoners, left them to die, with little food or water and no way to escape. Those arriving from Auschwitz and other camps did not even have a place to sleep. For nearly three months, until the British liberated Bergen-Belsen, the inmates languished in a nightmarish world: "We saw skeletons walking," says Renee Salt, all of sixteen at the time. "Their arms and legs were like matchsticks. . . . The stench that arose from the camp was terribly overpowering. It seemed that, after all we've been through already, this was something new and horribly different."[79]

The difference included a breakdown in order, as the Nazis either saved themselves by escaping or kept but minimal order in a camp populated with the weak, the starving, and the dying. Then, on April 15, 1945, British tanks rolled into Bergen-Belsen, liberating the living dead.

What Bergen-Belsen's suffering prisoners could not know was that Himmler, the mastermind of the camps, freely gave up the camp to the Allied forces. Although Hitler ordered the camp destroyed, Himmler, for once, did not obey his orders. Instead, he began making concessions with the enemy, allowing some Jews safe transport to Switzerland, for a fee, and freeing others and sending them to Poland.

"If I could have a fresh start," Himmler now admitted to a colleague, "I would do many things differently now. But as a loyal soldier I had to obey, for no state can survive without obedience and discipline."[80] His sentiment would be echoed by many of his Third Reich colleagues after the war.

But despite his previously unwavering loyalty to the Führer, Himmler wanted to save himself most of all. "He harbored the notable illusion," writes Ian Kershaw, "that the enemy might overlook his part in the monstrous crimes against humanity."[81]

While Himmler dreamed of escape, SS units were already throwing down their weapons and surrendering all across Europe. Alone in his private bunker in Berlin, Hitler realized that his dream of a united and victorious Reich, one he had once bragged would last one thousand years, was finished. Himmler's apparent betrayal may have been the last straw. According to Kershaw, "the bunker reverberated to a final elemental explosion of fury. All [Hitler's] stored up venom was now poured out on Himmler in a last paroxysm of seething rage."[82]

Hitler and his wife, Eva Braun, committed suicide on April 30, 1945, at 3:30 P.M. He could hear the tanks of the So-

German dictator Adolf Hitler and his mistress, Eva Braun, married on April 29, 1945, the day before they committed suicide.

viet army as they moved on the Reichstag. In his final note, he blamed the Jews for causing the war.

The End

Himmler wasted no time in making his intentions clear. During a final meeting at the Muerwick Navy School in northern Germany, he spoke to his SS commanders of disappearing into the countryside and ordered them to do the same.

His cowardice stunned Rudolf Höss: "This was the farewell message from the man to whom I had looked up so much, in whom I had had such firm faith, and whose orders, whose every word had been gospel to me."[83]

Two weeks later, Himmler was captured by British troops. He wore an eye patch as a disguise and was trying to cross a bridge at Bremervorde, Germany, into Switzerland. At first the two army sergeants who interrogated him thought him to be a low-level SS man. His papers identified him as Heinrich Hitzinger.

But after taking him to an internment camp, the British forces soon realized whom they had in custody. They searched him and discovered two vials of cyanide—a form of the gas the Nazis used to kill so many people— and removed them. But days later, before army doctors could examine him,

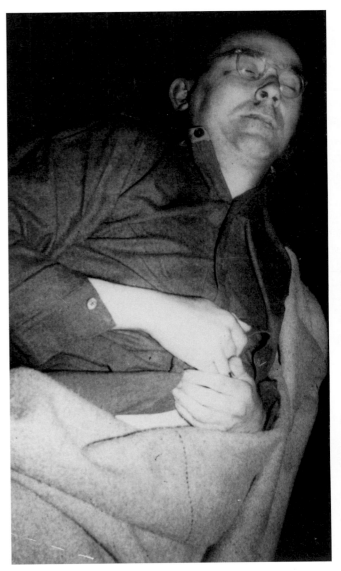

The body of German SS leader Heinrich Himmler is shown here after he committed suicide by biting down on a cyanide capsule.

Himmler bit down on a cyanide capsule lodged in his teeth and killed himself on May 23, 1945.

This official story notwithstanding, researcher Martin Allen recently claimed that Himmler was murdered by British intelligence before his negotiations with them were revealed. The truth of Himmler's death may never be known.

The Beginning

In November 1945 British Jewish publisher Victor Gollancz wrote of the Holocaust:

"I am never likely to forget the unspeakable wickedness of which the Nazis were guilty. But when I see the swollen bodies and living skeletons in hospitals here and elsewhere . . . then I think, not of Germans, but of men and women. I am sure I should have the same feelings if I were in Greece or Poland. But I happen to be in Germany, and write of what I see here."[84]

He was not alone in his utter horror at what had taken place. The troops that liberated the camps, including Auschwitz, discovered scenes that made their hair stand on end. But this was no movie. Around them were piles of bodies; ovens still filled with the ash from the corpses; starving men, women, and children. Disease ridden and barely alive, these survivors now had to somehow piece their broken lives back together. But could they return to countries like Austria, Lithuania, Hungary, and Poland without fear of further anti-Semitism? Many survivors were not so sure.

In Poland, such fears were warranted. Those who did return were vic-

Among the prisoners the Soviet army found during their liberation of the Auschwitz camp in January 1945 were scores of children, including this group.

timized once again in violent pogroms. The worst occurred in 1946 in the village of Kielce. There, unruly crowds murdered forty-two Jews and injured scores of others.

Ruth Webber remained embittered "toward everybody" by her wartime experience. "How they allowed me to, to be, to go through such misery for so long. . . . I was terribly angry at everything and everybody. Because nobody even cared after I survived, that I survived."[85] She was not alone in her feelings, but as the days passed, most people realized they had to go on living somehow.

Thousands of survivors tried moving west to France, Great Britain, and Belgium, among others places. Temporary refugee centers were set up in places such as Bergen-Belsen. These centers were run by the newly formed United Nations Relief and Rehabilitation Administration. The armies of Great Britain, France, and the United States helped organize and maintain them.

Other organizations like the American Jewish Joint Distribution Committee supplied Holocaust survivors with clothing and food, as well as offered job training. Sh'erit ha-Pletah, or "Surviving Remnant," a group dedicated to helping people find homes around the world, worked to help Jews immigrate to other countries. But options were limited at first.

The Jewish Brigade Group formed an organization to send displaced European Jews to Palestine in the Middle East. Yet British authorities in control of the region did not allow the exodus, in one instance turning back the ship *Exodus 1947* with forty-five hundred Holocaust survivors on board.

In December 1945 American president Harry S. Truman eased restrictions on wartime immigrants, thus ushering in over 41,000 people to the United States. Of these, 28,000 were Jews. Three years later the U.S. Congress passed the Displaced Persons Act, which subsequently brought 400,000 more refugees from Europe into the country. Other nations aided the effort, too, including New Zealand, Mexico, South Africa, Canada, and Australia.

Then, in 1948, after much political maneuvering and the displacement of thousands of Palestinians, the state of Israel was established. By 1953 at least 170,000 Jews had immigrated to what they considered their historic and spiritual homeland.

Sam Spiegel, who entered the United States in 1947, still thinks of his experience in Auschwitz and the promise he made with his fellow inmates: "We knew that a war . . . does not go on forever. And we . . . promised each other that somebody has to stay alive to tell what was going on in that hell, what really was going on in those camps and everywhere else. And in another short time, there's very few of us going to be left."[86]

Nuremberg: The Trial of the Century

The question remains: Did the Allied powers—the United States, Great Britain, and the Soviet Union—know about the

David Irving: Holocaust Denier

David Irving began his career as a historian in the early 1960s, but before long his work came under intense scrutiny. In subsequent works he argues that Hitler did not authorize and knew nothing about the "Final Solution." Later, Irving claimed the murder of millions of Jews is overstated and that gas chambers did not exist in Auschwitz: "There is no significant residue of cyanide in the brickwork," he said.

In 1996 Irving filed a libel suit against scholar Deborah Lipstadt, claiming she had defamed him by calling him a Holocaust denier. Irving represented himself at trial but was quickly overwhelmed with the defense's expert testimony. Cambridge professor Richard J. Evans, after much study, writes of Irving's work: "Not one of [Irving's] books . . . can be taken on trust as an accurate representation of its historical subject. All of them are completely worthless as history . . . if we mean by historian someone who is concerned to discover the truth about the past . . . then Irving is not a historian."

In the end, the trial judge sided with Lipstadt: Irving was a Holocaust denier. Irving, forced under British law to pay the courtroom costs, soon after filed for bankruptcy, his reputation as a historian ruined.

Quoted in Errol Morris, "Mr. Death," transcript, 1999. http://errolmorris.com/film/mrd_transcript.html.

Richard J. Evans, "David Irving, Hitler and Holocaust Denial: Electronic Edition, by Richard J. Evans," in *Holocaust Denial on Trial*, Emory University. www.holocaustdenialontrial.org/trial/defense/evans.

death camps before they liberated them? The simple answer is yes, the Allied powers knew about much of what was going on as early as December 17, 1942. That day, they issued the first joint declaration declaring their knowledge of the mass murder of European Jews and their intentions of prosecuting those responsible for war crimes. Less than a year later, in October 1943, foreign secretaries representing the three nations signed the Moscow Declaration. This pact stated that at war's end those believed responsible for war crimes would be returned to those countries in which the crimes had been committed.

When the war did end, these agreements enabled the wheels of justice to begin spinning in only a matter of months. Thus, between October 18, 1945, and October 1, 1946—less than three months after the official end to

World War II—one of the world's first war crimes tribunals began in Nuremberg, Germany. Its main defendant, Hermann Göring, had been Hitler's second in command and led the Third Reich's secret police known as the Gestapo. Confident by nature, Göring sneered at the proceedings. He and eighteen others were charged with crimes against humanity.

World War II had taken the lives of 55 million people over six years. The Nazis' "Final Solution" had been directly responsible for between 12 and 14 million of those. Five to six million were Jews; 1.5 million of those were under the age of fourteen.

U.S. chief prosecutor Robert Jackson, on leave from his position as associate justice of the U.S. Supreme Court, spoke of the charges being leveled against the defendants: "The wrongs which we seek to condemn and punish have been so calculated, so malignant and so devastating, that civilization cannot tolerate their being ignored because it cannot survive their being repeated."[87] Jackson's burden of proof was not very high: The defendants were hated, and their conviction was expected. Jackson also had plenty of hard evidence: The Nazis kept meticulous records of deportations and methods of destruction. As prosecutor Whitney Harris discovered: "I visited many Gestapo offices," he said, "and I found documents lying around on the floor, saying 'this many should be executed.' And I picked them up off the floor."[88]

Hermann Göring, Adolf Hitler's second in command, testifies at the Nuremberg Trials.

Nevertheless, tying specific Third Reich officials to particular crimes proved tricky, so instead, Jackson attempted to prove premeditation and prejudice against the Jews. He also intended to directly link Göring to their destruction. But the arrogant Gestapo leader did not budge, simply claiming that the trials were part of the spoils of war: The victors take revenge on the vanquished.

For four months the trials dragged on. At times tedious, at other times tense, Jackson and his fellow prosecutors built their case, piece by piece. One of the more telling moments occurred when film footage taken at the death camps was shown in court. It was the first time that the media and the public were given a glimpse at the horror of the Holocaust. As for the defendants, newscaster Walter Cronkite says that as soon as they saw the pictures, "they began to wither. As a matter of fact several of them cried. They weren't crying, I don't think, for the Jewish people that were lost. They were crying because they knew that, when those pictures were seen in the world they had no way to escape execution."[89]

Göring, though, remained calm and collected. On the day he took the witness stand, it appeared that his demeanor and his unwillingness to cooperate might save him. As five hundred spectators watched, Göring and Jackson battled for the upper hand. For his part, Göring claimed that the actions he took during the war were done simply to protect his country. He masterfully presented himself as a loyal and patriotic German, sacrificing himself for the good of his homeland and its people.

But five days into Göring's testimony, the sharp-minded Jackson tried a different tack:

Jackson: "You, Herman Göring, published a decree, imposing a fine of a billion marks for atonement on all Jews?"

Göring: "I have already explained that all these decrees at that time were signed by me and I assume responsibility for them."

Jackson: "It was you, was it not, who signed a decree to make plans for a complete solution of the Jewish question. That document is signed by you, is it not?"

Göring: "That is correct."[90]

Göring—under intense questioning—admitted his part in the "Final Solution." Other testimony followed, but the fate of Göring and ten other defendants was soon sealed. The verdict: guilty. The punishment: hanging.

Göring committed suicide by biting a cyanide capsule two hours before his death sentence was to be carried out. In a last letter to his wife he wrote, "I decided to take my own life, lest I be executed in so terrible a fashion by my enemy."[91] In this final decision of his life, Göring took a liberty he had helped deny to so many.

Unlike Göring, one high-profile war criminal escaped justice. Auschwitz's "Angel of Death," Josef Mengele remained a fugitive long after World War II ended. His twisted brand of medicine accounts for some of the worst atrocities committed during World War II. In 1949, after keeping a low profile in Europe, Mengele fled to Argentina. There he made a living carrying out illegal abortions and eventually buying a large share of a pharmaceutical company. He later went into hiding and, with help of family and friends, eluded justice. After an exhaustive investigation, authorities discovered Mengele's remains in 1985. He had died on February 7, 1979.

The Commandant Speaks

Rudolf Höss, the quiet and deliberate commandant of Auschwitz, initially escaped from authorities. As the Red Army moved on the death camp, Höss fled into Germany and lived under the assumed named of Franz Lang. But in 1946 he was discovered by Allied military police and handed over to Polish officials. His trial began in Warsaw, Poland, on March 11, 1947. The auditorium in which it was held was packed with journalists and Auschwitz survivors.

Like so many of his fellow Nazis, Höss said that he simply followed the orders given him; therefore, others, not he, were responsible for the suffering and death of so many. When he took the stand at the Nuremberg Trials, interpreter Joseph Maier says, "There was no emotion."

It was what he called a hard duty. He took no pleasure from it. . . . I

said "Didn't you have fun doing that?" I wanted to test him and see whether he was a sadist. He was no sadist. He was perfectly normal. He was doing his duty. He was doing his . . . believed he was doing his duty . . . he shut his eyes to the abnormality of this kind of thing he was doing, to the abyss, the incredible abyss to which human beings can descend in order to perform duties of that sort."[92]

Now, as he again sat on the witness stand, this time in the trial that would mean his life or death, Höss showed no sign of nervousness or fear. His deposition at the trial, translated into English and signed in Höss's own hand, recounts in some detail the Third Reich's greatest crimes as well as Höss's involvement. He denied little but wrote that he sometimes did feel queasy sending children to the gas chambers: "I did . . . always feel ashamed of this weakness of mine after I talked to Adolf Eichmann. He explained to me that it was especially the children who have to be killed first, because where was the logic in killing a generation of older people and leaving alive a generation of young people who can be possible avengers of their parents."[93]

Höss was sentenced to death in 1947 and returned to Auschwitz. Former inmates asked the court to carry out the sentence on the grounds of the death camp. The court agreed. The hanging, scheduled for April 14, 1947, was postponed, however, so officials could take measures to prevent citizens of Oświęcim from lynching Höss themselves.

At dawn on April 16, German POWs built the gallows. Höss arrived under armed guard at 8 A.M. and was taken to the building in which he formerly worked at Auschwitz. He drank a cup of coffee and spent his last hours in the "bunker," the former "Block 11."

At 10 A.M., his hands cuffed behind his back, Rudolf Höss strode one last time down the camp's main street. From here he could see the prisoner barracks, the gas chambers, and the crematoria.

Gallows were set up at Auschwitz to be used to execute former camp commandant Rudolf Höss on April 16, 1947.

Contemporary Hatred of Jews

Although the crimes of Auschwitz and the Holocaust are long past, anti-Semitism against Jews did not end in 1945. In 1972, less than thirty years after the end of World War II, the Olympic Games were held in Munich, Germany. The Germans viewed the event as a chance to restore their reputation and show the world their country had changed since the fall of Nazism. But on September 5, five Arab terrorists in track suits calling themselves Black September stole into the Olympic village and took eleven Israeli athletes and coaches hostage. Longs hours of negotiations between German officials and Black September ended when the terrorists were flown, with their hostages, to the Munich airport. Upon arrival, shots were fired, grenades were thrown, and all eleven athletes were murdered. Decades after the massacre in Munich, the scourge of racial anti-Semitism remains alive and well. Upon his election to the presidency of Iran in August 2005, Mahmoud Ahmadinejad stoked controversy when he announced that Israel "must be wiped off the map." He also claimed the Holocaust never took place. Ahmadinejad's comments were widely condemned, but his refusal to recognize the state of Israel has won him millions of admirers in the Middle East.

BBC, "Iran Leader's Comments Attacked," October 27, 2005. http://news.bbc.co.uk/2/hi/middle_east/4378948.stm.

Once he had ruled this sterile domain. Now he would be its last casualty.

Black-hooded executioners helped Höss onto a small stool placed beneath the swinging noose and the trap door. At 10:08, as a Catholic priest recited the last rites, a hangman kicked the stool from beneath Höss; his feet popped the trap door, and his legs swung free in the brisk morning air. He was pronounced dead at 10:21.

Five days before his execution, Höss wrote a letter to his children, which in part reads,

Your daddy has to leave you now. . . . The biggest mistake of my life was that I believed everything faithfully which came from the top. . . . Walk through life with your eyes open. . . . Don't just let your mind speak, but listen above all to the voice in your heart. . . . Have . . . soft and feeling hearts. Retain these throughout your later life. This is the most important thing. Only later will you understand that and will you remember my last words.[94]

Epilogue

"Reckoning II"

On August 20, 1965, hundreds of spectators and TV cameras from all around the world watched and waited. The Auschwitz trial at the Haus Gallus in Frankfurt had consumed more than a year's time, ranging over the course of 182 sessions. Witnesses to the horror of the Nazis' largest death camp had lashed out, broken down, and quietly recounted their experiences and confronted the SS guards and officials responsible for their nightmare. Although death sentences were unlikely, German attorney general Fritz Bauer's work had enabled victims to achieve some sort of justice.

Seventeen of the twenty defendants were found guilty of murder or aiding murder, although most received only modest jail time. But victims had confronted their persecutors and told the world their stories.

Today, the remains of Auschwitz are visited each year by thousands of tourists. They stream through the infamous gates, tour the empty barracks, peek inside the administration buildings, and march in silence through reconstructions of the gas chambers and crematoria. The death camp is now a museum, but all these years later at least one question remains: What was it like in Auschwitz? Hans Hofmeyer, presiding judge at the Frankfurt Auschwitz Trial, attempted an answer:

Above the camp gate it read "Work Will Make You Free." Between the lines it meant, "Abandon all hope, all ye who enter here." Beyond this gate began an inferno the normal human mind cannot begin to conceive of and no words can ever describe. The poor people herded into the camp were not only robbed of all possessions. The men, women and children were deprived of their hair. . . . The poor souls were goaded until they

Auschwitz survivors are shown in their barracks shortly after the Soviet army freed them.

dropped of exhaustion, which gave sufficient reason to beat them half or fully to death. Physically and mentally broken, the inmate was disrobed. Humbled, naked victims breathed their last miserable breath in Birkenau's gas chambers. Jews and Christians. Poles and Germans. Russian POWs and "gypsies." People from all over Europe. All some mother's child, each endowed with a human face.[95]

Notes

Introduction: "Reckoning"

1. Quoted in *Verdict on Auschwitz: The Frankfurt Auschwitz Trial 1963–1965*, dirs. Rolf Bickel and Dietrich Wagner, First Run Features, 1993.

Chapter One: Ashes to Ashes: The Origins of the "Final Solution"

2. Laurence Rees, *Auschwitz: A New History*. New York: Public Affairs, 2005, p. 49.
3. Rees, *Auschwitz: A New History*, p. xix.
4. Ian Kershaw, *Hitler, 1889–1936: Hubris*. New York: W.W. Norton, 1998, p. 100.
5. Kershaw, *Hitler, 1889–1936: Hubris*, p. 31.
6. Quoted in PBS, *The Great War and the Shaping of the 20th Century*. www.pbs.org/greatwar/historian/hist_wohl_06_hitler.html.
7. Ron Rosenbaum, *Explaining Hitler*. New York: Random House, 1998, p. 324.
8. Yehuda Bauer, *Rethinking the Holocaust*. New Haven, CT: Yale University Press, 2001, p. 32.
9. Quoted in Jeffrey Herf, *The Jewish Enemy: Nazi Propaganda During World War II and the Holocaust*. Cambridge, MA: Belknap Press of Harvard University Press, 2006, p. 23.
10. Quoted in David J. Hogan, ed., *The Holocaust Chronicle*. Lincolnwood, IL: Legacy, 2007, p. 86.
11. Quoted in Hogan, *The Holocaust Chronicle*, p. 86.
12. Quoted in Hogan, *The Holocaust Chronicle*, p. 103.
13. Quoted in Rita Thalmann and Emmanuel Feinermann, *Crystal Night*. New York: Holocaust Library, 1972, p. 42.
14. Quoted in Thalmann and Feinermann, *Crystal Night*, p. 49.
15. Quoted in United States Holocaust Memorial Museum, "Johanna Gerechter Neumann Describes Kristallnacht in Hamburg." www.ushmm.org/wlc/media_oi.php?lang=en&ModuleId=10005201&MediaId=1158.
16. Quoted in Thalmann and Feinermann, *Crystal Night*, p. 11.
17. Quoted in Robert C. Self, *Neville Chamberlain*. Hampshire, UK: Ashgate, 2006, p. 369.
18. Quoted in United States Holocaust Memorial Museum, "William (Welek) Luksenburg Describes the First Night of the German Invasion of Poland." www.ushmm.org/wlc/media_oi.php?lang=en&ModuleId=10005137&MediaId=1231.
19. Quoted in PBS, *The Great War and the Shaping of the 20th Century*.
20. Quoted in Rees, *Auschwitz: A New History*, p. 38.

Chapter Two: From Barracks to Death Camp

21. Klaus P. Fischer, *The History of an Obsession: German Judeophobia and the Holocaust*. New York: Continuum, 1998, p. 217.
22. Quoted in Eleanor H. Ayer, *In the Ghettos: Teens Who Survived the Ghettos of the Holocaust*. New York: Rosen, 1999, p. 24.
23. Saul Friedländer, *The Years of Extermination: Nazi Germany and the Jews, 1939–1945*. New York: HarperCollins, 2007, p. 92.
24. Daniel Jonah Goldhagen, *Hitler's Willing Executioners: Ordinary Germans and the Holocaust*. New York: Knopf, 1996, p. 149.
25. Quoted in United States Holocaust Memorial Museum, "Frima Laub Describes the Roundup of Jews for Mobile Killing Unit Massacre." www.ushmm.org/wlc/media_oi.php?lang=en&ModuleId=10005130&MediaId=1131.
26. Quoted in Rees, *Auschwitz: A New History*, p. 46.
27. Quoted in Rees, *Auschwitz: A New History*, p. 47.
28. Quoted in Rees, *Auschwitz: A New History*, p. 8.
29. Rees, *Auschwitz: A New History*, p. 20.
30. Friedländer, *The Years of Extermination*, pp. 339–40.
31. Quoted in Friedländer, *The Years of Extermination*, pp. 339–40.
32. Rees, *Auschwitz: A New History*, p. 79.
33. Quoted in Holocaust Education & Archive Research Team, "Paul Blobel," 2007. www.holocaustresearchproject.org/einsatz/blobel.html.
34. Quoted in Robert Jay Lifton, *The Nazi Doctors*. New York: Basic Books, 2000, p. 63.
35. Quoted in Laurence Rees, *Auschwitz: The Nazis & the "Final Solution."* London: BBC Books, 2005, p. 71.
36. Quoted in Yitzhak Arad, *Belzec, Sobibor, Treblinka*. Bloomington: Indiana University Press, 1999, p. 9.
37. Rudolf Hoess, Primo Levi, and Constantine Fitzgibbon, *Commandant of Auschwitz*. New York: Sterling, 2000, p.123.
38. Quoted in Rees, *Auschwitz: A New History*, p. 97.

Chapter Three: Factory of Death

39. Quoted in Goldhagen, *Hitler's Willing Executioners*, p. 105.
40. Quoted in Goldhagen, *Hitler's Willing Executioners*, p. 105.
41. Quoted in Friedländer, *The Years of Extermination*, p. 491.
42. Quoted in Toby Axelrod, *In the Camps: Teens Who Survived the Nazi Concentration Camps*. New York: Rosen, 1999, p. 45.
43. Quoted in *Verdict on Auschwitz*.
44. Leo Schneiderman, "Leo Schneiderman Describes Arrival at Auschwitz, Selection, and Separation from his Family," United States Holocaust Memorial Museum. www.ushmm.org/wlc/media_oi.php?lang=en&ModuleId=10005189&MediaId=1174.
45. Cecilie Klein-Pollack, "Cecilie Klein-Pollack Describes Arrival at Auschwitz," United States Holocaust Memorial Museum. www.ushmm

.org/wlc/media_oi.php?lang=en& ModuleId=10005189&MediaId=1106.

46. Quoted in PBS, *Auschwitz: Inside the Nazi State*, 2004–2005. www.pbs.org /auschwitz/about/transcripts_3.ht ml.

47. Gretchen Engle Schafft, *From Racism to Genocide*. Champaign: University of Illinois Press, 2004, p. 172.

48. Miklos Nyiszli, *Auschwitz: A Doctor's Eyewitness Account*. New York: Arcade, 1960, 1993, p. 62.

49. Sam Itzkowitz, "Sam Itzkowitz Describes Gas Chambers in Auschwitz," United States Holocaust Memorial Museum. www.ushmm .org/wlc/media_oi.php?lang=en& ModuleId=10005220&MediaId=1217.

50. Quoted in *Verdict on Auschwitz*.

51. Quoted in *Verdict on Auschwitz*.

52. Rees, *Auschwitz: The Nazis & The "Final Solution,"* p. 79.

53. Quoted in Gideon Greif, *We Wept Without Tears: Testimonies of the Jewish Sonderkommando for Auschwitz*. New Haven, CT: Yale University Press, 2005, p. 16.

Chapter Four: Surviving Auschwitz

54. Quoted in Primo Levi, *Survival at Auschwitz*. New York: Simon & Schuster, 1996, p. 41.

55. Quoted in Axelrod, *In the Camps*, p. 48.

56. Quoted in Deborah Dwork and Robert Jan Van Pelt, *Holocaust: A History*. New York: W.W. Norton, 2003, p. 367.

57. Quoted in Rees, *Auschwitz: A New History*, p. 254.

58. Quoted in PBS, *Auschwitz: Inside the Nazi State*.

59. Quoted in *Verdict on Auschwitz*.

60. Rees, *Auschwitz: A New History*, p. 175.

61. Quoted in Rees, *Auschwitz: A New History*, p. 183.

62. Quoted in Rees, *Auschwitz: A New History*, p. 184.

63. Quoted in Rees, *Auschwitz: A New History*, p. 84.

64. Quoted in Rees, *Auschwitz: The Nazis & The "Final Solution,"* p. 79.

65. Quoted in Rees, *Auschwitz: The Nazis & The "Final Solution,"* p. 258.

66. Quoted in Rees, *Auschwitz: The Nazis & The "Final Solution,"* p. 258.

67. Quoted in Rees, *Auschwitz: The Nazis & The "Final Solution,"* p. 258.

68. Quoted in Rees, *Auschwitz: The Nazis & The "Final Solution,"* p. 258.

Chapter Five: Liberation and Aftermath

69. Quoted in Friedländer, *The Years of Extermination*, p. 648.

70. Quoted in Rees, *Auschwitz: A New History*, p. 263.

71. Benjamin Ferencz, "Benjamin (Beryl) Ferencz Describes Collecting Evidence of Death Marches," United States Holocaust Memorial Museum. www.ushmm.org/wlc/me dia_oi.php?lang=en&ModuleId=100 05168&MediaId=284.

72. Quoted in Ian Kershaw, *Hitler. 1936–1945: Nemesis*. New York: W.W. Norton, 2000, p. 819.

73. Rees, *Auschwitz: A New History*, p. 271.

74. Bart Stern, "Bart Stern Describes How He Survived to Be Liberated in Auschwitz," United States Holocaust

Memorial Museum. www.ushmm. org /museum/exhibit/focus/auschwitz.

75. Sam Itzkowitz, "Sam Itzkowitz Describes the First Moments of Liberation." United States Holocaust Memorial Museum. www.ushmm .org/wlc/media_oi.php?lang=en&M oduleId=10005131&MediaId=1218.

76. Quoted in Rees, *Auschwitz: A New History*, p. 260.

77. Pat Lynch, "Pat Lynch Describes Condition of Surviving Camp Inmates upon Liberation," United States Holocaust Memorial Museum. www.ushmm.org/wlc/media _oi.php?lang=en&ModuleId=10005 131&MediaId=2970.

78. Quoted in Rees, *Auschwitz: A New History*, p. 260.

79. Quoted in Rees, *Auschwitz: A New History*, p. 266.

80. Quoted in Kershaw, *Hitler, 1936–1945: Nemesis*, p. 819.

81. Kershaw, *Hitler, 1936–1945: Nemesis*, p. 819.

82. Kershaw, *Hitler, 1936–1945: Nemesis*, p. 819.

83. Quoted in Rees, *Auschwitz: A New History*, p. 261.

84. Quoted in Kershaw, *Hitler: 1936–1945 Nemesis*, p. 840.

85. Ruth Webber, "Ruth Webber Describes the Bitterness She Felt After the End of the War," United States Holocaust Memorial Museum. www .ushmm.org/wlc/media_oi.php?lang =en&ModuleId=10005129&MediaId =1206.

86. Sam Spiegel, "Sam Spiegel Describes Reflections on Survival During the Holocaust," United States Holocaust Memorial Museum. www .ushmm.org/wlc/media_oi.php?lang =en&ModuleId=10005129&MediaId =3704.

87. Quoted in PBS, *American Experience: The Nuremberg Trials*. www.pbs.org /wgbh/amex/nuremberg/filmmore /pt.html.

88. Quoted in PBS, *American Experience: The Nuremberg Trials*.

89. Quoted in PBS, *American Experience: The Nuremberg Trials*.

90. Quoted in PBS, *American Experience: The Nuremberg Trials*.

91. Quoted in PBS, *American Experience: The Nuremberg Trials*.

92. Joseph Maier, "Joseph Maier Describes Former Auschwitz Commandant Rudolf Höss at Nuremberg," United States Holocaust Memorial Museum. www.ushmm.org/wlc/ media_oi.php?lang=en&ModuleId= 10005140&MediaId=1154.

93. Quoted in "Rudolf Höss," *Jewish Virtual Library*. www.jewishvirtual library.org/jsource/biography/Hoess .html.

94. Quoted in "This Is Rudolf Hoess' Final Letter to His Four Children," Lest We Forget. www.deathcamps .info/Letters/new_page_1.htm.

Epilogue: "Reckoning II"

95. Quoted in *Verdict on Auschwitz*.

Glossary

Arbeit macht frei: A slogan placed at the entrances to a number of Nazi concentration camps, most famously at Auschwitz. Translated into English from German, it means "Work Brings Freedom" or "Work Makes (one) Free."

Canada: A section of Auschwitz-Birkenau where prisoners' possessions—clothing, money, jewelry—were taken for sorting and shipment to Germany.

crematoria: The buildings in which murdered Auschwitz prisoners' bodies were burned in large ovens.

Einsatzgruppen: Paramilitary groups operated by the SS to kill Jews, Gypsies, and Soviet political prisoners.

gas chamber: The primary means of death at Auschwitz in which as many as four hundred prisoners at a time were packed tightly into a room and murdered with cyanide gas.

gestapo: The secret police of Nazi Germany, run by the SS, or *Schutzstaffel*.

Kapos: SS-appointed prisoners who were made to organize and discipline groups of camp workers.

selection: The process Auschwitz prisoners faced upon arriving at the camp, during which most were deemed unfit to work and sent immediately to the gas chambers.

Sonderkommando: A group of prisoners assigned to collect belongings and dispose of the bodies of other prisoners who had died or been killed.

SS, or *Schutzstaffel*: An important Nazi military organization that carried out much of the genocide at Auschwitz and other concentration camps during World War II.

Third Reich: A synonym for Germany during the Nazi regime.

Zyklon B: A commercial form of hydrocyanic acid, or cyanide, which became active on contact with air. It was manufactured by a firm called Degesch, which was largely owned by I.G. Farben. It was brought to Auschwitz in 1941 as a vermin killer and disinfectant.

For Further Reading

Books

Toby Axelrod, *In the Camps: Teens Who Survived the Nazi Concentration Camps*. New York: Rosen, 1999. This book provides a unique perspective on the Holocaust. Each of the brief anecdotes is told from the point of view of a young person who suffered through life in the ghettos or Auschwitz or was separated from his or her family.

Livia Bitton-Jackson, *I Have Lived a Thousand Years: Growing Up in the Holocaust*. New York: Simon Pulse, 1999. Bitton-Jackson's harrowing memoir of her experience as a thirteen-year-old in Auschwitz is hard to put down and harder to forget. She writes of her deportation and life in the notorious camp and how she and her mother will each other to survive and escape the gas chambers.

Anne Frank, *Anne Frank: The Diary of a Young Girl*. New York: Bantam, 1993. For those who have yet to read this classic account, Frank's diary provides a window into life during wartime that has yet to be surpassed. In simple, sweet prose, Frank chronicles the highs and lows of her time hiding in Nazi-occupied Amsterdam with her family.

Olga Lengyel, *Five Chimneys*. Chicago: Academy Chicago, 1995. First published in 1947, Lengyel's account of life at Auschwitz includes an up-close encounter with Josef Mengele as well as the tragic loss of her husband, two sons, and parents.

Primo Levi, *Survival at Auschwitz*. New York: BN, 2007. Beginning with Levi's deportation from Italy, *Survival* takes readers on a straightforward and gut-wrenching journey into the heart of darkness. Few survivor accounts are as well written and moving as this one.

Elie Wiesel, *Night*. New York: Hill and Wang, 2006. Elie Wiesel's harrowing account of his life before and during his imprisonment at Auschwitz provides a moving firsthand account of the Holocaust. The book's brevity and directness is a perfect introduction for many young readers.

Allan Zullo and Mara Bovsun, *Survivors: True Stories of Children in the Holocaust*. New York: Scholastic, 2004. This book includes shattering accounts of survival under the most difficult circumstances. Profiling nine Jewish boys and girls from across Europe, Zullo chronicles great escapes, wrenching separations, and a desperate desire to live.

Web Sites

The Anne Frank House Museum (www .annefrank.org/content.asp). If you have read the diary of the world's best-known victim of the Holocaust, you will find this museum and its Web site a crucial supplement to your study. Aside from a history of the house and the Frank family's secret stay there, the museum has an abundance of photographs and letters.

Auschwitz-Birkenau (www.auschwitz.org.pl). If you are planning a trip to Poland or simply want more information on the infamous death camp, visit this thorough and easy to navigate site. Here you can also read a detailed history of the camp and view photographs of the crematoria and barracks from the air.

The Holocaust History Project (www.holocaust-history.org). This storehouse of documents, essays, and photographs related to the Holocaust is a solid starting place for research into the twentieth century's greatest crime. The Web site also includes firsthand information such as crematoria timesheets written by members of the Third Reich.

Images for Reflection (www.imagesforreflection.com). Photographer Scott L. Sakansky recently traveled to most of the concentration and death camps run by the Nazis, and he brought back pictures. His Web site contains the haunting result: hundreds of color and black-and-white photographs that stand as a testament to the Holocaust.

Simon Wiesenthal Center (www.wiesenthal.com). Simon Wiesenthal (1908–2005) made it his life's work to track down and bring to justice Nazi war criminals. Today, the organization he founded continues the hunt and has expanded its mission to fight genocide and injustice throughout the world.

United States Holocaust Memorial Museum (www .ushmm.org). One of the first stops for any serious student of the Holocaust is this elegantly organized but painfully truthful history of what Jews refer to as *Shoah*, or "calamity." Located in Washington, D.C., it not only contains thousands of archives related to those who perished but has on display actual artifacts. Included in the collection is a boxcar used to convey people to the death camps and four thousand pairs of shoes left behind by those sent to the gas chambers at Majdanek.

USC Shoah Foundation Institute (www .college.usc.edu/vhi). The Shoah Foundation Institute of the University of Southern California was started by filmmaker Steven Spielberg after his experience directing the Holocaust drama *Schindler's List* in 1993. The Web site allows viewers to listen to first-person testimonies of Holocaust survivors.

Index

Picture Credits

About the Author

David Robson is a playwright, freelance writer, and English professor. He is the recipient of two playwriting fellowships from the Delaware Division of the Arts, and his work has been performed across the country. Robson is also the author of many books for young readers on subjects ranging from the Kennedy assassination to the Black Arts Movement. He lives in Wilmington, Delaware, with his family.